AMERICAN MOVIES
AND THEIR CULTURAL ANTECEDENTS
IN LITERARY TEXT

AMERICAN MOVIES AND THEIR CULTURAL ANTECEDENTS IN LITERARY TEXT

Phebe Davidson

Studies in the History and Criticism of Film
Volume 4

The Edwin Mellen Press
Lewiston•Queenston•Lampeter

Library of Congress Cataloging-in-Publication Data

Davidson, Phebe.
  American movies and their cultural antecedents in literary text / Phebe Davidson.
    p. cm. -- (Studies in the history and criticism of film ; v. 4)
  Includes bibliographical references and index.
  ISBN 0-7734-7342-4
  1. African Americans in motion pictures. 2. Women in motion pictures. 3. Motion
pictures and literature. I. Title. II. Studies in history and criticism of film ; v. 4.

PN1995.9.N4 D38 2001
791.43'6520396073--dc21

2001031250

This is volume 4 in the continuing series
Studies in the History and Criticism of Film
Volume 4 ISBN 0-7734-7342-4
SHCF Series ISBN 0-7734-9734-X

A CIP catalog record for this book is available from the British Library.

The Edwin Mellen Press
Box 450
Lewiston, New York
USA 14092-0450

The Edwin Mellen Press
Box 67
Queenston, Ontario
CANADA L0S 1L0

The Edwin Mellen Press, Ltd.
Lampeter, Ceredigion, Wales
UNITED KINGDOM SA48 8LT

Printed in the United States of America

To Tom Mack

Contents:

Preface: Playing on the Other Side   i
Josephine A. Koster

Foreword: Reading a New Art   v

Acknowledgements   viii

Introduction: Looking through the Windows   1

Seeing in Black and White: Suppressed Racial Violence   9
From *The Defiant Ones* to *The Green Mile*

Good and Guilty Narratives: the White Man Speaks—   27
Samuel Clemens, John Sayles, and *The Brother from
Another Planet*

"History with Lightning":   47
The Legacy of D.W. Griffith's *The Birth of a Nation*

When Rubber Meets the Road: *Thelma and Louise*   67
and *Leaving Normal* as Complementary Cultural Texts

Will the Real Fairy Godmother Please Stand Up?   85

Dead Already: Fathers and Anti-Feminism   105
in Three 1999 Films

Index   129

Preface:
Playing on the Other Side

Josephine A. Koster

With my typewriter, the text is at a distance; it is visible and I can work with it. With the screen, it's different; one has to be inside; it is possible to play with it but only if one is on the other side, and immerses oneself in it.

—*Jean Baudrillard*

As I write this preface, Brian May's brilliant soundtrack to Alexandre Aja's debut feature-length film *Furia* is pulsing on the stereo; the screenplay to Kevin Smith's *Dogma* lies open on my table. The distance between these two films—one a passionate allegory of the silencing of postcolonial dissent in Algeria, the other the director's quirky "love letter to God" (00) and deconstruction of the nature of belief—is paralleled in *American Movies and Their Cultural Antecedents in Literary Text,* an eclectic and insightful look at the ways race, gender, and identity are handled (or mishandled) in American film. Aja, the French *enfant terrible* and son of famed French auteur Alexander Arkady, uses the story of two graffiti artists (Theo and Elia) and the government's persecution of them for writing and drawing anti-government themes on the walls of a conquered city to argue forcefully for the artist's right to total freedom of expression, despite the conventions and needs of the larger society. Smith, the Orson Welles of Red Bank New Jersey, equally as emphatically argues that the ways we see our beliefs—whether they be about the forgiveness of sins or the gender and racial identities of God, Christ, and the original apostles—*must* be placed in a social frame and in the long track of history. That two films made by young, intelligent, talented directors in the same year can take such different stances tells us something of the conflicted and diverse views in modern cinema. Phebe Davidson in *Six Essays* probes deeper into that conflict.

Like Aja and Smith, Davidson's means of exploration are novel. This may be the first time in modern film criticism that *Calvin and Hobbes* has been used to interrogate Richard Donner's *Lethal Weapon* films and Fenimore Cooper's Chingachcook simultaneously. Davidson confesses that "I have been a voracious (if not always discriminating) reader from childhood to present" (73); and the range of her viewing reflected in this collection is encyclopedic. Here we have informed readings of works as old as *The Birth of a Nation* and as recent as *The Green Mile*, as well recognized as *American Beauty* or as little known as *Pinky* and *Limbo*. The juxtapositions can be startling, as in the case of Fenimore Cooper and *The Brother from Another Planet* or the Brothers Grimm and *To Wong Foo, Thanks for Everything! Julie Newmar*, yet always they seem familiar, well grounded in common sense and perceptive observation.

When Davidson digs deeper into what she calls the question of "good and guilty narratives" (19), her ability to separate the filmmakers' motives and the outcomes of their efforts shines lucidly through. In her reading of *Birth of a Nation*, for instance, she points us accurately to Dixon's and Griffith's use of title cards to reinforce belief, silence dissent, and create a monocular interpretation; as she says, "Prior to *The Birth of a Nation*, the world had not yet fully envisioned the power of feature length movies to sway the emotions or even their power to attract audiences" (55). Her reading points to both the good and guilty outcomes of such filmmaking. Likewise, when she connects Ridley Scott's *Thelma and Louise* with the genre of captivity narratives, Davidson radically shifts our views of what might easily be dismissed as a male attempt to write a female "buddy movie" so that we see it as a rejection, rather than reification, of the conventions of the genre. When she contends that "the literary underpinnings of a narrative may be almost invisible because they derive from textual material that has been metabolized by the culture at large to such an extent that it has become part of an invisible substratum of cultural knowledge" (75), we are inclined to agree because of the wide range of knowledge she herself brings to bear on the essays—everything from the 1812 edition of *Grimm's Fairy Tales* to the most recent of Disney renderings.

At times, one is tempted to argue with some of Davidson's readings; for instance, she contends that "Butch and Sundance choose their mode of life largely out of a sense of boredom with civilization" (60), an assertion somewhat at odds with George Roy Hill and William Goldman's statements that the story is about two men knowing their world has changed but not knowing what to do about it (DVD); the comparison of the generation disillusioned by Vietnam and the generation after the Civil War would certainly politicize the erstwhile bank robbers' motives as much as it does those of Thelma and Louise. But it is hard to argue with either the confidence or the humor of a critic who can write that "Cinderella's elevation to royalty, however, makes it shiningly clear that certain behaviors, in the long run, are ruinous to young women" (102).

Throughout, Davidson's *Six Essays* make clear that she has, as Jean Baudrillard argues, learned to place herself on the other side of the screen from these texts. Seeing them as she does, from her oppositional perspective, she opens up these movies to us as both viewers and critics. Unlike Calvin's father, who thinks his son sees the world only in black and white, Davidson helps us see these movies in a much richer, more vibrant perspective. And she needs to: for as Calvin says, "SOMETIMES THAT'S THE WAY THINGS ARE!" (3)

Rock Hill, SC

January 2001

Works Cited

Hill, George Roy, dir. *Butch Cassidy and the Sundance Kid (Special Edition)*. DVD
   Edition. Twentieth-Century Fox, 2000.

May, Brian. *Furia: Soundtrack to the Film by Alexandre Aja*. London: EMI, 2000.

Smith, Kevin. *Dogma: A Screenplay*. London: Faber & Faber, 2000.

Thibaut, Claude. "Jean Baudrillard on the New Technologies: An Interview with
   Claude Thibaut." *Cybersphere 9: Philosophy* (March 3, 1996). 28 January
   2001 <http://www.uta.edu/english/apt/collab/texts/newtech.html. >

Foreword:
Reading a New Art

Phebe Davidson

The history of the movies is, first of all, the history of a new art.

—*Gerald Mast and Bruce Kawn*
A Short History of Film

As a child, I spent my Saturday afternoons at the movie theater—*The Liberty*—in the town where I grew up. The Saturday matinee cost a quarter and included cartoons, previews of coming attractions, and selected shorts as well as a feature film. From my parents' perspective, I suppose these junkets offered a good bit for the money they cost. From my perspective as a viewer, they offered endless delights of a sort not readily available at home, books, the nine inch black and white TV, and an assortment of board and card games notwithstanding.

Those trips to the movies became an integral part of my life, shaping not just my Saturday afternoons but the ways in which I saw and framed the world. They taught me to be a patriot, to value sacrifice, to count the value of true love, to recognize horror . . . and as a Saturday matinee devotee I didn't think much about the meaning of what I saw. My gut-level understanding of World War II, like my students' understanding of the Vietnam War, comes not from a study of history or the reading of novels, nor even from the stories told by uncles who had served, but from the movies. Movies have, far more than I have always been willing to admit, shaped what I know and what I believe.

If the movies are a new art—and they are certainly that, still evolving into new forms and narrative strategies, embracing new technologies that continue to alter the product we call film—they are nonetheless rooted deeply in the culture that continues to produce them. What has come to fascinate me as an adult is the persistent recurrence in popular movies of stories and themes that have been evolving in the American cultural ethos since well before the Revolution, the same stories and themes that have both moved (and been carried by) American literature and art into each new century. More and more, I am conscious of these other stories that lie just beneath the surface of the stories I am watching on the big screen.

These essays come from my love for the layered cultural texts that I know as the movies. The discussions are wide ranging, representing some effort to track the evolving presentation and understanding of stories and themes in different media and different periods of time. They are also exploratory, an exercise in seeing where a particular idea, image, or sequence of events will lead. Since the movies are in some sense shadows of the very culture they shape in turn, these essays are a way for me to see the film in broader contexts than I otherwise might, an enterprise I hope will be rewarding to others as well as to myself.

Aiken, SC

January 2001

Work Cited

Mast Gerald and Bruce Kawn. *A Short History of Film.* Boston: Allyn and Bacon,
  2000

Acknowledgements

Grateful acknowledgement is made to the following publications in which earlier versions of two of these essays appeared:

> "Seeing in Black and White: Suppressed Racial Violence in Trans-Racial Buddy Movies." *Social Sciences and Humanities Journal.* XXX. 1999-2000. 35-43.

> "Will the Real Fairy Godmother Please Stand Up?" *Film and Literature: Points of Intersection.* Edwin Mellen Press: 1997.

Photo Credits:

> Carmike Cinema. Aiken, South Carolina by Steve Davidson. Used by permission.

> Author photo by Todd Lista.

The author extends her gratitude to the friends and colleagues who have extended their interest and support in the preparation of this manuscript and to Steve Davidson for his invaluable assistance. Special thanks also to Josephine A. Koster for her helpful reading and for "Playing on the Other Side."

Introduction:
Looking through the Windows

*Of all the products of popular culture, none is more sharply
etched in our collective imagination than the movies.*

—*Steven Mintz and Randy Roberts*
Hollywood's America: United States
History Through Its Films

Audiences experience entire films, not snippets.

—*David Bordwell and Kristin Thompson*
Film Art: an Introduction

What is it about the movies? We go to see them and, if they work as well as
they should, they stay with us. In some instances, we even become aware of images
from movies we have never seen and respond to them in particular ways. Thus,
"(e)ven people who have never seen *Citizen Kane* or *Casablanca* or *The Treasure of
the Sierra Madre* respond to advertisements, parodies, and TV skits that use these
films' dialogue, images, and characters" (Mintz and Roberts 1). One need not be
tremendously movie oriented to be heavily influenced by the versions of life that
appear on the silver screen; it is enough merely live and breathe in a culture of which
the movies have become a vibrant part. As art and entertainment, our movies reflect
American life and American concepts of everything from politics to romantic love to
just about anything you care to name. These same movies also shape American life

and beliefs to an as yet unmeasured extent. Whether our concern is the effect on young children of screen violence, the understanding many of today's moviegoers have of America's involvement in Vietnam, or even the nature of love, the movies have had an impact on the way we think about things. For these reasons, if for no others, the movies themselves bear thinking about.

About ten years ago, I realized that after I had watched a movie I felt as if I had sampled a dish that was inexplicably rich in flavor. For hours afterward, to extend the metaphor, I was tasting—or at least remembering the flavor and texture—of things that I had been unconscious of at the time of the meal. This happened with movies in general, regardless of the overall quality of the film. *Something* in the movies was always teasing at the back of my mind, distracting me from other pursuits. These essays represent my effort to understand what in the movies accounts for that sensation. My method has been to track associations that I find between a given film (or group of films) and residual areas of my own knowledge.

American culture as I know and understand it has always been animated by the issues of race and gender.[1] The reasons for this are complex but not difficult to understand. The new world that was colonized by Europeans seemed, to many of them, to be a truly virgin territory, an empty land on which they could impress their visions of reality and from which they could draw sustenance and even riches without hindrance. These immigrants embodied a broad spectrum of desires that ranged from sufficient land to sustain a family to religious freedom, from the establishment of great estates and mercantile powers to the freedom to journey endlessly through the wilderness, from a longing of younger sons to be what they could not in Europe (propertied, titled, powerful, respected . . .) to the simple desire to conquer and exploit.

---

[1]Both of these are inextricably tied to the question of social class, but nonetheless remain as distinct issues in a culture that frequently likes to imagine that it is immune to class considerations.

European settlers of the lands that eventually became America developed powerful myths and narratives of their own, many of which are so deeply engraved on the American consciousness that by now they have become a sort of psychological baseline in American thinking. Such narratives include stories of journeys into the wilderness (in America closely linked with coming-of-age), of outlaws-on-the-run, and of the settlement of new lands.

Because America became an experiment in political egalitarianism, the individual has come to assume more importance than had been the case in those European societies from which so many immigrants came. One consequence is that America has spent upwards of two centuries redefining the meaning of humanity, in part by expanding that meaning to include former slaves and women. So doing, American thought and society have engaged two of the most powerful and enduring issues in American culture—race and gender. These issues, even today, illuminate the thinking of Americans about themselves and their places in the world..

As a reader, I am particularly conscious of cultural narratives as they are expressed in texts that range from the earliest American writings, largely non-fiction, to the novels of the twentieth century. As a movie goer, I cannot escape their presence in film. The lingering flavors that I detect after a movie are, after all, only the stories that lie beneath the surface of the film's narrative. These are often stories that the culture has been telling itself since colonial days, stories that represent the culture's effort both to justify itself and to understand itself in the context of its growth and development.

The essays in this book try, for the most part, to assess the narrative content of various movies by reading them through their literary predecessors in American culture. Social realities and historical circumstance, however, also shape the content of film.[2] Since literature, like film, is to some extent a reflection of the culture that

---

[2]For example, *The Birth of a Nation* reflects very specific racial attitudes and deliberately manipulates audience perceptions of history while *American Beauty, The Sixth Sense,* and *Limbo* take their life from a deeply rooted contemporary concern

4

makes it, there should be no surprise that the enduring themes of race and gender are often the focus of American movies. Of these two themes, race supplies the focus of the first three essays while the second three are more concerned with gender.

"Seeing in Black and White: Suppressed Racial Violence from the Defiant Ones to the Green Mile," for example, discusses four movies *(The Defiant Ones, Die Hard, Lethal Weapon,* and *The Green Mile)* in the context of a popular American cartoon strip, *Calvin and Hobbes,* as well as in the context of such literary antecedents as James Fenimore Cooper's *Leatherstocking Tales* and Mark Twain's *The Adventures of Huckleberry Finn.* This approach reveals significant continuities in American narrative practice as well as in social attitudes.

Similarly, "Good and Guilty Narratives: the White Man Speaks—Samuel Clemens, John Sayles, and *The Brother from Another Planet,*" explores John Sayles' 1984 film, *The Brother from Another Planet,* in the context of American slave narrative. The appropriation of a black man's story by a white author carries some risk as an authorial practice, risk that figures separated as widely by time and social circumstance as Sam Clemens and John Sayles have managed in tellingly similar fashion.

Given the racial focus of the first two essays, it seemed appropriate to include as well a less literarily nuanced effort, "'History with Lightning': The Legacy of D.W. Griffith's *The Birth of a Nation.*" This famous (and infamous) epic marked the advance of D.W. Griffith into the front ranks of American filmmakers. Because the film is based to a large extent on racist attitudes and historical misrepresentations, specific literary texts are less relevant than the broad tradition of plantation fiction with its enduring racial stereotypes. The power of Griffith's film to sway social thinking reminds contemporary viewers that it has not yet lived out its cultural life and that the movie, if it is to be understood as a cultural document, demands a broadly contextual examination.

---

about the role of fatherhood in American society.

The fourth essay in this collection marks a shift in thematic focus. "When Rubber Meets the Road: *Thelma and Louise* and *Leaving Normal* as Complementary Cultural Texts" is primarily concerned with gender. The essay examines these two feminist buddy/road movies as examples of different genres. Though both movies encapsulate the journey into the wilderness, they are very different kinds of stories. The first (*Thelma and Louise*) is a mythic journey of the sort engaged upon by Huck Finn and Jim, by Butch Cassidy and the Sundance Kid, and by such earlier American figures as Mary White Rowlandson. The second film (*Leaving Normal*) is a fairy tale. Analyses of these two films, grounded in literary text, do much to account for their difference in narrative posture and cultural meaning, along with explaining why one film is so much more disturbing than its very similar counterpart.

"Will the Real Fairy Godmother Please Stand Up?" continues to trace the importance of fairy tale in American popular culture, following the operation of the fairy godmother figure in a 1949 social issues film, *Pinky*,[3] and 1995's gender-bending comedy, *To Wong Foo, Thanks for Everything, Julie Newmar*. These two movies, their theatrical releases separated by 46 years, delineate dramatic shifts in the way American filmmakers have been able to configure and reconfigure gender and gender roles on screen.

The final essay in the collection, "Dead Already: Fathers and Anti-Feminism in Three Films from 1999" discusses the less obvious underlying themes of three movies—a suburban dark comedy (*American Beauty*), a thriller (*The Sixth Sense*), and an adventure-survival story (*Limbo*)—reading them as anti-feminist responses to social and cultural pressures that have altered the traditional concept of fatherhood in America. That the same anxiety expresses itself in such different genres argues a strong concern in the culture at large about the question of masculinity and fatherhood as they have been conventionally understood.

---

[2]As a social issues or "message" film, *Pinky* marks an intersection of race and gender in popular culture. Though the focus of "Will the Real Fairy Godmother Please Stand Up?" is gender, race is impossible to ignore in this quintessentially American movie.

6

The readings contained in this book are not intended to be definitive. They are offered as interpretive exercises that may enrich the understanding of a movie by suggesting new angles of vision and new contexts in which to think about its content. Because cultures, like the individuals who inhabit them, change and grow in ways that are sometimes unpredictable, any effort to affix a final meaning to a cultural text is impractical in the extreme.

I believe, along with Steven Mintz and Randy Roberts, that "As cultural artifacts, movies open windows into American cultural and social history" (1). These essays come of looking through those windows.

Works Cited

Bordwell, David and Kristin Thompson. *Film Art: an Introduction.* 3rd edition. New
York: McGraw Hill, 1990.

Mintz Steven and Randy Roberts. *Hollywood's America: United States History
through Its Films.* USA: Brandywine Press, 1993.

Seeing in Black and White: Suppressed Racial Violence
From *The Defiant Ones* to *The Green Mile*

Do you leave a light on after bedtime? Because I get
a little scared in the dark sometimes. If it's a strange place.

—*John Coffey*
The Green Mile

In 1999 Castle Rock Films released *The Green Mile*, the second prison drama written by Stephen King and directed by Frank Darabont. The movie tells the story of John Coffey, a black man convicted of the molestation and murder of two little white girls and condemned to death. Imprisoned on Death Row in Louisiana's Cold Mountain Penitentiary in the summer of 1935, Coffey is the catalyst that makes the film's story line possible. His interactions with and effect on the white characters who surround him are profound and, as it works out, derive much of their energy and importance from the fact that these characters are prison guards and other condemned men—all white—whose lives and understanding of the world they inhabit are irrevocably changed by their experience of John Coffey. Curiously and significantly, this movie set squarely in the American justice system makes surface gestures toward questions of justice and race, but at the same time avoids any deep involvement with these issues. In particular, the movie fails to address, on any but the most superficial terms, the issue of justice and its failures in a racist society.

To understand how this is possible, one needs to take a fairly deep look at racial narratives that are embedded in American culture. These narratives, particularly as they have been inscribed by white men, reflect considerable discomfort and "disease" with the white man's position of power in the new world represented by precolonial and colonial America. Coupled with this discomfort is the white man's unwillingness to relinquish or renegotiate that position. The source of this problematic set of narratives can be found in the treatment by whites of their darker counterparts, particularly native Americans and blacks, during the construction in North America of the United States. Failure to recognize this and its implications for contemporary narratives is a denial of reality.

Let me begin with a *Calvin and Hobbes* cartoon by Bill Watterson. In this seven frame strip, little Calvin is trapped in a sequence of six black and white drawings. He discovers that "the world has no hue, value, or chroma" (Watterson 148). He tries to account for this with various hypotheses, always referring to himself in the third person. Thus he distances himself, as it were, from the terrifying immediate problem that is loss of color or, seen from another angle, of suddenly restricted vision. He wonders,

> Have the photo receptors in Calvin's eyes stopped working properly, or has the fundamental nature of light changed? Perhaps some strange nuclear or chemical reaction on the sun has caused electromagnetic radiation to defy separation into a spectrum! Maybe objects no longer reflect certain wavelengths! (Watterson 148)

Clearly, Calvin is acutely distressed by the phenomenon and anxious to discover its cause. On one point he is absolutely without doubt. "Whatever the cause, it's clear to Calvin that there's no point in discussing things with his Dad" (Watterson 148).

In the strip's seventh and final frame, in full color, we see Calvin's father saying "The problem is, you see everything in black and white" (Watterson 148). Small wonder Calvin was reluctant to include Dad in the discussion. Calvin's rather desperate reply, lettered in vivid scarlet, is "SOMETIMES THAT'S THE WAY

THINGS ARE!!" (Watterson 148).

One very serious implication of this comic strip is that people need to make a determined effort to see "the way things are," even when that seems to contradict the obvious surface of what is being looked at. If, unlike Calvin's father, we make a serious effort to see things in black and white, we can discover a great deal.

The phrase "black and white" has specific implications in print and in film, all related to Watterson's cartoon. To be accused of seeing things "in black and white" is to be accused of reductive reasoning, of failing to grasp the full (usually ethical or moral) complexity of an issue. We are also familiar with "in black and white" as the fine cliché that is often used to clinch an argument. There it is, *in black and white,* meaning, of course, that the ultimate authority of print, black ink on the white page, is irrefutable. Never mind the specious logic, the phrase has a ring.

With *Calvin and Hobbes,* however, we find ourselves looking at that marvelous art form, the comic strip, a series of pictures with dialog balloons. The cells of the strips are closely akin to the frames of a motion picture—each frame a still that advances both the narrative motion of the strip and the physical disposition of the elements of the frame and (in larger context) of the story itself. And we are, perforce, looking at it in black and white right up until the full color of the explosive last image. The irony of this colored final image with its brilliant scarlet text is obvious: All that vivid passion engendered by black and white.

If a film appears "in black and white" as opposed to color, the presumption frequently is either that the filmmaker is working on a low budget and cannot afford color film, or else that the simple elegance of black and white will present the elements of the picture with a sort of privileged clarity, leaving the audience undistracted by the effusion of cinematic color. The outcry against the colorization of "movie classics" by Ted Turner is a good example of the rhetorical and symbolic weight an audience can give to black and white even though that same audience may well demand the full barrage of color in its contemporary film fare. As an audience, we seem not to want to change the "complexion" of our narratives.

Still, as Bill Watterson (in fine angry scarlet) points out about black and white, sometimes we have to see things that way because that is, in fact, the way they are. A conscious effort to see in black and white reveals some interesting and telling continuities in American cultural treatment of the elements of black and white as they are (and have been) constructed within the society as a whole, particularly as the terms apply to race.

In American literature it has been the practice since at least James Fenimore Cooper's day to link the white, English-speaking hero with a darker double. In Cooper's case the link that is forged between white frontiersman Natty Bumppo and the Iroquois Chief, Chingachcook can be read without too much difficulty as an effort to morally and ethically justify the position of the white man in the American wilderness—to make him, in some way, the legitimate inheritor of the Indian he has displaced rather than a simple thief or a conqueror. This pattern of the doubled hero reappears in Mark Twain's *Huckleberry Finn* where it serves much the same purpose—the legitimization of the white "inheritor" of America by his association with his darker skinned companion, though in Twain's novel the whites have stolen not the darker man's land, but his very self. This linkage of the white-skinned hero with a black double sets a pattern that persists in popular culture, even now.

While the following is probably not a definitive reading of *Huck Finn*, it is certainly a useful one, and has for me the added merit of delineating certain enduring issues in American culture. In Twain's novel, we meet a white youngster, Huck, who is apparently motherless and who bears his drunken and abusive father's surname of Finn. Huck's story is cast as a journey, motivated in part by his love of adventure, but having as its articulated purpose an escape from the encumberments of civilization. In his search for freedom, Huck hooks up with a runaway slave, Jim. Together, the two set out into America in search of freedom and self realization.

Huck is a youth, friendless, fatherless—and white. Jim is an adult, fugitive, sensitive to the ties of family (he has one himself)—and black. As the episodic tale unfolds, Jim becomes the protector and moral mentor of Huck. At the novel's close,

Jim's rescue is engineered by the literarily minded but morally unformed Tom Sawyer, under whose direction Huck and Jim participate in a melodrama that results in the runaway slave's capture and, incidentally, in his injury. This seems poor payment for all Jim's goodness throughout the novel, and the revelation that he has been freed by his owner seems a rather thin addition to the plot.

Huck's desire to "light out for the territory," to escape the impending threat of becoming "civilized" is made credible and even admirable by the moral and ethical tutelage supplied by Jim as the two travel by raft down the Mississippi. On this voyage, the reader is invited (or inveigled) into seeing the complex and hypocritical world through the lively intelligence (and innocence and logical consistency) of a young boy. It is, rather obviously, important that Huck has no mother. His biological father, the notorious Finn, does not deserve his son. Huck's informally adoptive father, Jim, cannot claim him as a son. Nonetheless, Huck inherits the right to his own freedom from the flummery of civilization in a purely male line.

The nature of the family, in Twain's novel, is never explored. Those family units we do get to see are white and either incomplete, hideously self-destructive (as the Sheperdson-Grangerford feud demonstrates) or so easily duped as to be embarrassing. It is made painfully clear that the female sex (as exemplified by Widder Douglass) simply doesn't cut it when the task at hand is raising a man-child. Yet since Pap is unfit for the job, another must step in.[1] Given that Pap is a member of the unlettered working classes, it is singularly appropriate that another laborer should take his place. Behold, Jim.

Significantly, Jim is always "kept in his place" (and out of sight) by a combination of factors. One is that he is terrified of discovery. Another is that he has no desire to overstep his place with Huck or any other white. Thus, his freedom

---

[1]Pap Finn, the drunken Irish day laborer, is representative of a popular American stereotype and a fairly obvious representation of the unwelcome working class immigrant. Though not a major character, and conveniently killed off well before the novel's close, he nonetheless introduces in the novel an element of class bias that is rarely noted.

(should he get to realize that condition) in no way threatens to impinge on white privilege.

Jim's attachment to family, moreover, feminizes him in a cultural sense, establishing in him an appreciation for the domestic hearth that is unparalleled in Huck Finn's youthful heart. By contrast, Huck's efforts to disguise himself as a girl fail to feminize the young white male, who is easily detected as a disguised masculine presence. Hence, many pages later in the tale, it is perfectly appropriate for Jim to return home to domestic concerns and for Huck to head west, striking out into the American continent as the legitimate inheritor of the American estate. Much of white reading America apparently found these circumstances regarding the two characters not merely palatable but righteously convincing for close to a century.[2] As recently as 1999, the same could be said of many American moviegoers.

To a remarkable extent, American narratives and American audiences are haunted by Huck and Jim. This same pair, whether designated as black and white buddies or as hero and sidekick, appears again and again in American cinema, almost always as a pair of fugitives. Of the two, one of is a rogue while the other is more stable, more firmly rooted in the values of the larger community. Almost invariably, despite the historical evidence that he would have received less reward for these qualities, this role is filled by the black partner. It is the black partner who "domesticates" or softens the character of his white colleague. At the same time, it is the white partner's affection for his companion that legitimizes the relationship of the two, or at least this is the perception of a primarily white audience. If there is any sexual interaction with a woman, it nearly always involves the white partner, and it

---

[2]The novel was not the only burgeoning genre in nineteenth-century America. The slave narrative (as exemplified in the work of Frederick Douglass and Harriet Jacobs) was also exceedingly popular. This form detailed the events of a slave's successful flight to freedom and to selfhood. It is worth mentioning that in *Huck Finn* we have, at least in part, the appropriation by a white author of this quintessentially African American genre as we are taken on the slave's journey to freedom through the eyes of a largely unschooled white boy.

never destroys the bond between the two men. Indeed, the affection of the two men for each other can be seen as the whole point of the narrative.

One variant on Huck and Jim appears in Stanley Kramer's 1958 *The Defiant Ones*, which pairs Sidney Poitier and Tony Curtis as black and white convicts Noah Cullen and John "Joker" Jackson. In this movie the audience learns quickly that the pair despise one another.[3] When Noah Cullen and "Joker" Jackson escape from imprisonment, they are literally chained to each other. By the time they rid themselves of the chain, their hatred has been transmogrified into mutual respect and something that, if it is not quite friendship, is extremely close to it. Kramer's efforts at social realism, which appear rather heavy handed and self-indulgent at the remove of nearly forty years, were pretty strong for their time.

The black and white male pair personified by Joker and Noah was, in 1958, discomfiting to moviegoers and critics in more ways than one. While both figures are adult males, it is the white "Joker" played by Tony Curtis who gets involved with the woman, just as it had been the white Huck who interacted with women (and others) in Twain's novel (and as it is Christopher Lloyd's character in *T-Bone & Weasel* and so on). In Huck's case, given his age, this means primarily that as the white male, he is the one empowered to deal with the outside world. In the case of Joker Johnson, this automatic prerogative is expanded into the adult arenas of sexual and romantic encounters.

Jim's social invisibility relative to Huck can be laid at the door of his fugitive condition. To be sure, Huck is also on the run. As a white male, however, he has much greater range in society at large than does Jim. Additionally, Jim is on the run

---

[3]This is a variation on the black-white relationship Twain's novel. In the case of Huck Finn, his status as a child protects him from any racial animosity on Jim's part, partly because Jim is a decent man and partly, as we later learn, because he is a father. This makes the symbolic fatherhood assumed by the black man both reasonable and agreeable to readers. In Kramer's film, the paternal relationship of the black man to the white is made clearest is the closing shot, in which the seated Noah Cullen (Sidney Poitier), singing defiantly, holds and supports the injured Joker (Tony Curtis) as they look up at the lawmen who will take them back to prison.

from the law while Huck is merely on the run from his father, a matter of domestic rather than criminal weight. The same reasoning doesn't exactly fit in a situation where the white man and the black are *both* fugitives from the law. In order for the narrative to make sense, the audience must buy into the film's suggestion that the problem is the racist south which is, if one looks at the pre-figuring narratives, merely a symbol for a racist nation.

The Defiant Ones brought to the attention of its contemporary viewers the nearly hopeless quality of such a transracial friendship in American society. One of the movie's most moving scenes takes place after the chain has been severed. Noah Cullen (Poitier), has caught a train and Joker Johnson (Curtis), is running, trying to catch up so that the pair can make a symbolic rail journey into America in some kind of voluntary companionship. While this might seem, on the surface, to be a desirable outcome, it is not an outcome that was universally trusted or desired. As Thomas Cripps reports in *Making Movies Black*, there were a number of fans who "as the Poitier character . . . leaned over from his perch on a moving train to help the white convict to whom he had been chained, shouted 'Get back on the train, you fool!'" (292). Nonetheless, the movie closes with the pair reunited. Noah Cullen rejoins his fellow fugitive on foot, and at the movie's close has his arms around the injured Jackson, singing defiantly into the face of the white lawman who finally catches up with them.

Though a product of its era, *The Defiant Ones* acknowledged a racially based hostility that was, for Hollywood filmmakers as it had been for Twain, a dangerous thing indeed, likely to alienate the white middle-class audience at which both their works were directed. Consequently, this hostility was disguised as something else, usually an irritation and unease based on one character's impetus to action (Huck, Joker) and the other's to caution. This disguised racial tension would also make its presence known in such later action-adventure efforts as Warner Brothers' 1987 *Lethal Weapon* and its sequels and Twentieth Century Fox's 1988 *Die Hard*, which spawned its own train of sequels.

Other parallels with Huck and Jim also add force to the black and white male pairings in these films. In *Lethal Weapon,* directed by Richard Donner and released in 1987, Danny Glover's 50 year old police sergeant Roger Murtaugh is partnered with Mel Gibson's thirty year old homicide detective, Martin Riggs. Like Twain's Jim, Murtaugh will prove to be a domesticating (and saving) presence in Riggs' life. Like Huck, Riggs is the younger member of the duo, domestically as free as a bird. His wife, recently killed in an automobile accident, is apparently the only family he has ever had or cares about. Like Huck, he is an antic presence, given to quirky (and often humorous) foolhardy acts that make his partner acutely nervous. That the two men are opposites is underscored by their initials—M.R.(Martin Riggs) and R.M. (Roger Murtaugh)—each set of letters the reversal of the other.

The age difference between Roger Murtaugh and Martin Riggs is underscored by such factors as Murtaugh's insistence, when the duo is on the road, that *he* be the one to drive. Murtaugh makes it very clear that he hardly trusts Riggs, whom he considers crazy and possibly suicidal. But while Murtaugh drives the car for almost the entire film, Riggs gets to drive in the final confrontation sequence. Throughout the movie, in fact, Riggs drives the relationship. His emotional neediness (as well as his charm) gain him welcome in the Murtaugh family, which is as apple-pie wonderful as any nuclear American family since *Leave it To Beaver.*

Like Twain's *Adventures of Huckleberry Finn,* Donner's *Lethal Weapon* provides no glimpse of a functional white family. The closest the viewers come to seeing a white family at all is a look at Murtaugh's old war buddy Hunsacker, himself deeply involved in a heroin ring, whose porn star daughter has just killed herself. As the film's conflicts begin to unwind, we learn that Murtaugh owes his life to Hunsacker. Within the next forty-eight hours, he will also owe it to Riggs. The debt to Hunsacker is canceled by the combined weight of Riggs' heroism and Hunsacker's treachery.

Like Huck, Riggs is a focus for complexity. When Murtaugh, annoyed by Riggs' convoluted theory about a witness, asks "Why you gotta make things complicated?" Riggs' reply "That's the way things get all by themselves" (*Lethal Weapon*) is remarkably like Calvin's "THAT'S THE WAY THINGS ARE!" Like Calvin, Riggs is making a statement that serves as a metaphor for conditions of life, in this case both for his place in the film and for the confusing condition of a society that burdens the hardworking cop with such thankless and endlessly confusing dilemmas. Like Calvin in *Calvin and Hobbes* and like Huck in Twain's novel, Riggs seems to see the world around him clearly, without impediment.

If Riggs shares with Huck both the freedom of the unfamilied and an antic disposition, then Murtaugh must be acknowledged as sharing some of Jim's limitations as an actor in the world. Tied to family, ethical, reluctant to take any sort of violent action, he is an object of scorn to Riggs. Uncontained and self-destructive, Riggs is a danger to Murtaugh as fully as to himself. Yet when Murtaugh's daughter is kidnaped by Hunsaker and his crowd of villains, it is Riggs who must perform the rescue.

There is, to be sure, a tradition in which a romance would then blossom between Riggs and the daughter, but in this particular vision of America, what might be called the "Huck Finn vision," there is no room for such a relationship. To be sure, the daughter thinks Riggs is cute. But she is years too young for Riggs and is so terrified by her ordeal that she retreats to a position of absolute dependence on her father, voluntarily submerging her sexuality. She thinks of Riggs as unsuitably older than herself, apparently unaware of race as a possible issue, and Riggs apparently thinks of her as "just a kid." He is as blind as she is to the possible complications of interracial relationships. Thus, his inherent decency and her propriety combine to defuse a potentially explosive issue in the story. While the issue of interracial romance is denied visibility, the male relationship resumes its primacy in the story as Murtaugh and Riggs come to share a protective, paternal role.

And, indeed, how else could the matter be handled? If the romance were to blossom, then the close bonding of Murtaugh and Riggs would become the secondary relationship and the romance—the triumph of sentimental love—would emerge as the primary focus of the denouement. Murtaugh domesticates his partner. Riggs enlivens Murtaugh. As with Huck and Jim, the conjunction that matters is the conjunction of the two men, for that is what shapes their true identities and their destinies in the world.

This not very startling fact is equally true of *Die Hard,* directed by John McTiernan and released in 1988 by Twentieth Century Fox. In this movie, New York city detective John McClane (Bruce Willis) has flown to Los Angeles in an effort to effect a reunion with his estranged wife (Bonnie Bedelia) who has left him to pursue a career in the corporate world. The story is set on Christmas Eve in the new and extremely impressive Nakatomi building. The building is empty, save for the company party at which McClane's wife is present and except for the uninvited cohort of international thieves led by the enigmatic Hans (played by the nearly ubiquitous Alan Rickman) who become the partygoers' captors. And except, of course, for John McClane, who leaves the party where he is an awkward guest to enter the framework, ductwork and bowels of the building, a sort of contemporary variant of going underground, to save the woman he loves.

Like Riggs, McClane is domestically disconnected. Like Riggs, he is a rogue. Like Riggs, he is drawn back to his own humanity by a black man, Sergeant Al Powell (played by Reginald VelJohnson) whose pregnant wife awaits him at home. Al Powell serves as the only link between John McClane and the outside world for most the film's duration. Like Riggs and Murtaugh, McClane and Powell share the embrace that really matters at the movie's close.

Of these two films, Fred Pfeil has noted in *White Guys* that they valorize the working class male, a gesture that he reads as part of a larger backlash against the feminism of the preceding decade. He also notes, however, that the "the black man seems to receive from the white man's hands not only the capacity for effective violence, but something very like virility itself . . ." (13). By this he means that the black male is empowered by his association with the white male to act in public in ways that would otherwise not have been accepted, that might have been interpreted as simple savagery. Pfeil also notes that the black male offers what he calls "*gendered healing*. . .insofar as McClane's and Riggs's worst, most excessively male tendencies towards self-destructive behavior [are concerned]" by bringing them back to the pleasures of the hearth. He notes as well that both movies continue past their endings. Like Huck emerging from his journey on the mythic waters of the Mississippi, John McClane experiences a symbolic rebirth as he emerges from the guts of the Nakatomi Building.

The real closure, Pfeil tells us, comes with embrace of partners—Riggs falling backward into Murtaugh's arms after a prolonged fight with Gary Busey's villainous Mr. Joshua and John McClane's embrace of Al Powell *before* he hugs his wife and heads out of frame. On my own, I will add that those embraces alter irreversibly the nature of any embrace that either man may subsequently share with a woman, wife or otherwise. They are, in a curious way, an assault on the domestic hearth whose value the black men demonstrate for their white companions. These exclusively *manly* embraces insist that the hearth is now a shared, transracial male perquisite. The men, variously empowered by one another, are able to embrace women, if you will, as a secondary matter. In Pfeil's view, this is not just a sexist scenario, but a class one as well. All the men in question are, after all, "working stiffs."

In 1999, *The Green Mile*, has recreated Huck and Jim in yet another retelling of the forging of black and white male friendship in America—in this case returning us (as did *The Defiant Ones*) to the American south of the early twentieth century. As so easily happens within a culture or society, newer narratives contain the narratives that preceded them, modifying them to some extent, but also recapitulating those earlier stories. In American culture, for instance, these narratives, from James Fenimore Cooper's *Leatherstocking Tales* to Stephen King's *The Green Mile*, are about the bond of transracial male friendship. All, incidentally, are offered to the audience from a white point of view that presupposes a white, mainstream audience. Thus, the presence of an encoded tale of white racial guilt makes a good deal of sense. Huck Finn's tale may give us a white man's narrative, but a black man's experience as a slave on the run lies at the heart of the novel. *The Green Mile,* directed by Frank Darabont and released in 1999, adheres to the same pattern. The white narrative is the one we are given, though the experience of the black man lies at the story's heart.

Paul Edgecomb (Tom Hanks) is, like Riggs, McClane and so on, a working class man. Employed by the penal system, Edgecomb joins the gallery of law enforcement personnel that includes Detectives Riggs and McClane. Like them, Edgecomb is enlisted in retelling this story of transracial friendship. Edgecomb is given nearly godlike power as he supervises Death Row, the film's "green mile" of linoleum. His glaringly decent humanity undercuts the absolute quality of his power regarding the treatment and fate of the men awaiting execution. In fact, this overriding quality of decency apparently removes the sting of Edgecomb's power from the minds of fellow guards and prisoners alike.

The two exceptions in this orderly response to Paul Edgecomb are guard Percy Wetmore (Doug Hutchinson), and inmate William "Wild Bill" Morton (Sam Rockwell). Wetmore is a sadistic and finally deranged guard who covets power. Prisoner William "Wild Bill" Morton is the psychotic killer of two little white girls for whose sins John Coffey (Michael Duncan) has been condemned to suffer execution. Ultimately, Coffey will die for Rockwell's sin.

Where the film gets interesting, at least to me, is that it lobs some easy shots at racism in its presentation of John Coffey without ever landing a telling blow. The audience is offered a number of opportunities to affirm that this movie is not about race, but about human goodness and the ability to forgive. While forgiveness is generally an admirable quality, it serves in this instance to weaken the movie's moral stance regarding race.

Good John Coffey is unjustly condemned, largely because of his race. Yet the appalling effect on the audience of bigot John Hammersmith (Gary Sinese) is mitigated somewhat when the audience is shown his son's face, hideously scarred by a mongrel dog. The implication is that Hammersmith is drawing the wrong lesson from life's harsh realities, and he is made to some extent an object of pity. The audience is also confronted with Good John Coffee the Christ Figure, forgiving and healing his killers. If John Coffey forgives those who make his life so terrible, who are we to condemn them? If the movie is about race at all, the narrative seems to say, it is a condemnation of racism. We all end up loving John Coffey. What could be more of a challenge to racism than that?

The answer to that question lies in the movie's cultural subtext, which is somewhat more chilling than the movie's surface and which bears strong connections to earlier narratives of friendship between white and black men. Paul Edgecomb suffers from a urinary infection. John Coffey cures that infection by a laying on of hands and coincidentally imbues Edgecomb with increased sexual potency, so that Edgecomb's wife is satisfied "several times" (*The Green Mile)* by Coffey's healing ministrations. Whatever the intentions of the screenwriter and director, this sequence is a fairly obvious enactment of the myth of the power of black sexuality.

Coffey himself, as a black man, can only be *allowed* to touch white women in particular ways, specifically (in this film at any rate) in order to heal them. Edgecomb, realizing Coffey's healing power, takes him to minister to the dying wife of his supervisor. When he heals this deranged woman, John Coffey absorbs some very strong racially couched abuse from her. The audience has seen enough of Coffey's forgiving nature to assume that he blames not the woman herself but rather her disorder for the ugly, hurtful words she utters. Sure enough, once healed, she abandons the terms and beliefs of racial abuse. The implication that racism is not so much a social wrong as it is a disease and that like many diseases it is curable is not in itself offensive—but the implication that this is all there is to the matter is somewhat more so.

Just as Paul Edgecomb makes it possible for John Coffey to "lay hands on" a white woman, in her bedroom, at night for the sake of this healing, he makes it possible for the audience to understand that the circumstantial evidence that has made possible Coffey's conviction has been misinterpreted. When Coffey is found holding the bodies of two dead little white girls and weeping, he can only be understood by those who discover him to have touched them in very particular ways—as a sexual predator and killer. Yet the audience knows that when he found those small, dead, white girls, he held them in his arms in an effort to heal them. Despite his unusual powers, then, John Coffey is denied a real sexual identity of his own although he is allowed to bestow sexual potency on another.

In Cooper as in Twain, the troubling (if noble) "darker brother" in the text obligingly assumes his "rightful" position in the scheme of things of his own volition. In Cooper's *The Pioneers,* the aging Indian chief, last of his tribe, goes up to his mountain to die and leaves the American estate to Natty Bumppo, a frontiersman who is white but who has shared the Indian's relationship with the natural world. In Twain's *The Adventures of Huckleberry Finn,* Jim, upon learning that he is free, returns to his family, where he wanted to be all the time. The implication is that it wasn't slavery alone, or perhaps even primarily, that bothered him. Far worse was the threat of separation from his loved ones.

These generous (and sometimes incredible) attitudes of self-effacement are present in *The Green Mile* as well. John Coffey asks Paul Edgecomb not to interfere with his electrocution. He wants to die because his sensitivity to all the pain in the world is too much to bear. In the movie's narrative world, this is justification enough for the wrongful electrocution of the black hero. The innocent, childlike Coffey forgives all and obligingly absents himself from the scene of his humiliations. Coupled with John Coffey's lack of intellect, his childlike "innocence," makes of him, at least in the rather white perspective of the film's narration, the ideal African American.

Though there is some suggestion in the film, both through the use of the "J.C." initials and through Coffey's willingness to die for the sins of others, that he is to be viewed as a Christ figure, he doesn't quite achieve that status. It is difficult to see Christ in a man who confuses Fred Astaire and Ginger Rogers with angels in heaven. The filmmaker's choice of a Fred Astaire/Ginger Rogers dance number as the controlling vision of heaven is, in its way, perhaps the "whitest" moment in a tremendously white movie.

Far more effectively than he emulates Christ, John Coffey reinforces the persistent image of the hero's darker double, who willingly effaces himself in order to affect the legitimization of a white hero. The white hero, for his own part, is invariably allowed to slide off the ethical hook on which he might seem to be caught. Coffey, like Chingachcook, wants to die. Coffey also explains that he had to give Edgecomb "a part of myself" (*The Green Mile*) before he could let go. The Jims and John Coffeys will, as we are told over and over in these white stories about black men and white, fix whatever is broken, forgive their enemies, and (like Cooper's Chingachcook) voluntarily disappear, leaving the world to their white successors. The white successor, in all of these instances, has been legitimized by his darker "brother" through the darker man's teachings, his gift of sexual power, his relative closeness to the natural world, and most importantly by his forgiveness.

The pretense that color doesn't matter in an American movie is thin, to say the least. This is especially true when color is presented in terms of black and white, those loaded racial terms that have haunted American culture from its earliest days. To suggest, for instance, that *The Green Mile* is not a film about race, is nonsense. As Cindy Fuchs points out in her review of *The Green Mile,* John Coffey is defined in a peculiarly limiting way. "John's ordeals define him: He has no life other than what he means for Paul, a white man consumed by guilt and sadness" (2). The same observation holds true for the figures of Jim and Chingachcook, both of whom are pivotal figures in classic American novels, as it does for Noah Cullen, Al Powell, and Roger Murtaugh, equally pivotal figures in American movies of which the earliest discussed here, *The Defiant Ones,* had as at least part of its purpose a confrontation of racist stereotypes.

If we are to believe what these movies offer, the conjunction of black and white men in friendship remains very nearly as unsettling in America today as it was forty or one hundred or two hundred years ago. Whether transracial male bonding occurs in an action adventure movie or in a mawkish prison melodrama, the subtext is eerily persistent. The functions of domestic space and wildness show us a great deal about how much our popular culture relies on Huck and Jim to show us that they are still finding their way into America. There is an obdurate and wistful determination to present theirs as a hopeful journey, one that may yet bear the fruit of brotherhood and forgiveness, in spite of all the evidence to the contrary.

For the sake of argument, I will close by suggesting that while these particular texts and movies have latched onto the working class as part of the vehicle for Huck and Jim's continued journey into America, class continues to matter less in this pairing than gender and race. The Huck and Jim figures of black/white buddy and sidekick films are generally working class or, more recently, part of the underclass that forms a desperate culture of poverty and its attendant evils. This is nothing new. It is in fact what they always were. That this is an essential part of American cultural myth hardly needs explaining.

What is really significant, beyond what I see as the inevitability of their social class in popular narrative, is the cultural message of this pair about race as they move through movies on the order of *Salt & Pepper, White Men Can't Jump, Gridlock'd, T-Bone 'n' Weasel, Guys Like Us, Stir Crazy, White Nights, A Family Thing, The Fan, The Choirboys, Skin Game,* and even *Seven*[4]. The narrative point of view is persistently white. The audience is required to see John Coffey and his predecessors from the outside, from the point of view of a white author. One result is that these black characters remain opaque to the general, white audience. On the other hand, that same audience sees the white "heroes" from inside a shared cultural perspective. Because these narratives have been authored or appropriated by representatives of the dominant white culture, they promulgate the cultural filters of one culture at the expense of another. Like Calvin and his father in the Watterson's cartoon, we have an opportunity to see it all laid out in black and white. As we have already been reminded, sometimes that *is* the way things are.

---

[4]This is not to say that *all* movies featuring black and white buddies follow the same pattern. Some, like *Beverly Hills Cop* and *48 Hours* are inversions of the narrative discussed here.

Works Cited

Cripps, Thomas. *Making Movies Black*. NY: Oxford U. Press, 1993.

Die Hard. Dir. John McTiernan. With Bruce Willis, Reginald VelJohnson. Twentieth Century Fox. 1988.

Fuchs, Cindy. *The Green Mile*. www.citypaper.net/movies/g/greenmile.shtml. 2/17/2000.

Lethal Weapon. Dir. Richard Donner. With Danny Glover, Mel Gibson. Warner Bros. 1987.

Pfeil, Fred. *White Guys*. NY: Verso, 1995.

The Defiant Ones. Dir. Stanley Kramer. With Sidney Poitier, Tony Curtis. United Artists. 1958.

The Green Mile. Dir. Frank Darabont. With Tom Hanks, Michael Duncan, Michael Jeter, Sam Rockwell. Castle Rock Entertainment/Warner Bros. US. 1999.

Watterson, Bill. *The Calvin and Hobbes Tenth Anniversary Book*. Kansas City: Andrews & McMeel, 1995. 148.

**Good and Guilty Narratives: the White Man Speaks
Samuel Clemens, John Sayles
& *The Brother from Another Planet***

*A spaceship doesn't have to get hit by nothin' to crash.
Sometimes it gets internal malfunctions.*

—*Smokey*
The Brother from Another Planet

In American life and letters, as in American film, we are confronted again and again with issues that are in great degree political. Among these are the issues of race and of ownership—issues that have a connection so intimate as to be nearly identical. No one, I think, will argue that our nation lacks its full share of racial injustice, ranging from European colonization through chattel slavery to ensuing forms of repressive discrimination. Thus, African Americans have come to occupy a somewhat anomalous place in the literature of a country that once denied them literal self-possession. The possession of the African American's story, like the possession of the African American self prior to emancipation, is problematic. Two examples in particular, Mark Twain's *The Adventures of Huckleberry Finn* and John Sayles' *The Brother from Another Planet*, are cases in point. Both employ the classic slave narrative as a basis for their own narrative inventions.

Slave narratives were particularly important in America in the years preceding the Civil War, when questions of white supremacy and racial injustice divided the nation into bitterly opposed camps. These narratives, written or transcribed, were the stories of escaped slaves cast in the first person. Typically, a slave narrative related a series of events that included a slave's coming to understand the evil of slavery, the struggle to escape, and the achievement of freedom. Frequently the story ended in the newly free narrator's commitment to the abolitionist cause.[1]

Intended largely for an audience of non-slaveholding whites, these first person narratives added considerable fuel to the anti-slavery movement. The uses of the slave narrative in this political endeavor also created some ambiguity as to who actually "owned" those narratives—the narrators themselves or the abolitionists who edited, published, and made use of the stories. The enduring question has become, at least for me, not whether a writer or writer/director is entitled to use another's experience in the creation of work he or she will claim to own, but how such use affects the writer's position in relation to that story. If authorship is never easy, it is in some cases more complicated than in others.

This is particularly true in *The Brother from Another Planet*, an independent film by John Sayles. One of America's best known independent film makers, Sayles has generated a body of distinctive work that encompasses widely disparate visual frames. Thus, these movies range from the urban grit of *Return of the Secaucus Seven* to the Louisiana bayous of *Passion Fish* through the desolate coastal beauty of the north Irish coast in *The Secret of Roan Inish* to the desert and treacherous borders of *Lone Star*. What ties these films together? Sayles once said "My main interest is making films about people , . . . I'm not interested in cinematic art" (*Bio* 1). Though it is hard to know how this could be in a man who makes movies, the fact remains that

---

[1]The Abolitionist movement published slave narratives and promoted them extensively in order to enlist public support for the abolition of slavery. To this end, the editors and publishers of these narratives were extremely thorough in authenticating the material they published. Because a spurious narrative would have been ammunition for pro-slavery forces, it was crucial to publish narratives that were, in practical terms, unimpeachable. The two American slave narratives best known and most frequently studied are *The Narrative of the Life of Frederick Douglass, an American Slave*, originally published in 1845 and *Incidents in the Life of a Slave Girl*, published in 1861 by Harriet Jacobs under the pseudonym Linda Brent.

Sayles is certainly concerned with people and the issues that shape their lives.

In all his films, Sayle's draws on a degree of what might be called "outsideness" or alienation to develop his themes and *The Brother* is no exception. The movie is a bit unusual for Sayles in that it seems to relate very strongly to pre-existing literary works and even to replicate literary practice for both its content and its narrative strategy. It can be argued that Sayles goes out of his way to make this connection clear to viewers—something that suggests a consciousness on the film's part of its own *relative* position as an expression of specific concerns that are an inextricable part of American culture. Race is the overriding concern of this particular movie but other issues such as gender, police tactics, and drugs are also given attention.

The Brother from Another Planet derives from and closely imitates the American slave narrative, a form that virtually guarantees the racial focus of the film's narrative line. The focus on drugs, although it is something more than incidental, is introduced and developed through a night journey that seems to exist outside the narrative proper, a digression that needs to be considered both as part of Sayles' effort to redefine the slave narrator and as a reflection of an allusive sequence that is actually alien to the primary genre of slave narrative, drawing instead on poetry for its logic.

That "escaped slaves were writing for a white audience" (Sayre 164) illustrates in part how complicated authorship was for authors of slave narratives in the nineteenth century. For those who could not write their own stories, the influence of the amanuensis may well have presented difficulties of authorial control. Additionally, the narratives were shaped not only by the author's experience but by the sensibilities and experiences of the intended readers, who were for the most part white. Thus these narratives became reflections of America's idea of itself not only from the position of the African or African American slave but also from the position of both the free white readership and the numerically smaller free black readership which also existed.

Two of the best known America slave narratives, (*The Narrative of Frederick*

Douglass, An American Slave, Written by Himself, and *Incidents in the Life of a Slave Girl* written by Harriet Jacobs under the name of Linda Brent) demonstrate the importance of this form to America's concept of itself. As critic Robert F. Sayre points out, "... in black autobiography one constantly finds refutations of the white ideas of America, of both the white concepts of white characters and the white concepts of black" (165). It is important to recall that these refutations are often couched in such a way as not to alienate a readership composed primarily of whites whose sympathy the narratives seek to enlist.

Two very solid beliefs have kept the slave narrative, at least in critical perception, in the authorial hands of American blacks. One is that "No Black American author has ever felt the need to invent a nightmare to make his point" (Roger Rosenblatt 171). The other, as James Olney points out, is that "black history was preserved in autobiographies rather than in standard histories . . . because black writers entered into the house of literature through the door of autobiography" (Olney 15).

Slave narratives were undeniably the product and possession of those who had suffered slavery. Yet the central plot of those narratives has been appropriated in American culture by no less imposing a figure than Samuel Clemens. At the heart of *The Adventures of Huckleberry Finn* lies the narrative of a fleeing slave—Jim—whose story we are given through the eyes and voice of a white boy, Huckleberry Finn. Yet another slave narrative is enacted by John Sayles' *The Brother from Another Planet,* a film written, directed by, and acted in by its white creator. If this appropriation (by Clemens and by Sayles) is not entirely comfortable for me in my position as audience, neither is it deserving of absolute condemnation. In moral terms, both narratives come out largely on the side of the angels, and have the grace to exhibit for the perceptive a certain authorial uneasiness with their chosen narrative vehicles.

The Adventures of Huckleberry Finn, demonstrably an "anti-slavery" novel, was not published until 1885, well after slavery's end. The book uses the story of Jim, an escaping slave, to motivate the moral growth of Huck, a motherless white boy whose father is an abusive drunk. As Huck and Jim travel down river, Huck is the adventurer and Jim the figure in the shadows. Yet Jim is the adult and Huck is the child. When Jim finds the body of Huck's father on a wreck, he shields Huck from that knowledge. Though Jim must remain in hiding because of his fugitive slave status, he is nonetheless the balance for Huck's unpredictable whims and behavior.

Like Twain's novel, *The Brother from Another Planet* tells the story of a black man's flight to freedom. Also like Twain's novel, it was not forged in the anguish of a slave's experience. It was one result of a MacArthur Genius grant, awarded to Sayles in 1983, which provided him with something over $30,000.00 a year for five years, tax free. In *The Brother*, one sees some of the rough cinematic edges that are almost inevitable in a film by a relatively new film maker accustomed to low-budget work. Certainly, low-budget conditions were part of Sayles' working experience. 1978's *Secaucus Seven*, for instance, was shot in four weeks at a cost of $40,000 (Thomson 667; *Bio* 1). Sayles wrote *The Brother*, in fact, only when another project fell through.[2] Nonetheless, the movie reflects deep understanding of the racial issues at the heart of slave narratives written in an earlier span of history and argue Sayles' own familiarity with the genre.

The central character in *The Brother from Another Planet* is a stranger in America. He is a black man and he is mute. In this, he is like Huck's companion, Jim, who must remain effectively silent if he is to escape. He is also very like Frederick Douglass, a black man who struck north into America and freedom relying on two crucial sources of strength—the aid of strangers and his own resourceful intelligence. Douglass, like The Brother and like Jim, had no sure place in the scheme of things. Early in his post-slavery life, Douglass attracted the notice of William Lloyd Garrison who enlisted him as a speaker on the abolitionist circuit. Though impressed by Douglass's skill, his abolitionist mentors were not entirely willing to let Douglass tell

---

[2]*The Brother from Another Planet* came into being only after funding for *Matewan* fell through the first time leaving Sayles with $300,000.00 and a crew assembled to make a picture (*Bio.* 1).

his own story in his own choice of words. He was advised " 'to use a little of the plantation speech' rather than to seem 'too learned' " (Meyer xvi).

By his death, Frederick Douglass had become one of the great orators of his age, yet as an abolitionist speaker who was a fugitive slave, Douglass had been instructed to speak like a plantation hand. He was abjured not to use the educated speech of the day because that would lessen his credibility. Thus his voice was in some measure muted even in relative freedom. As a slave prior to escape, of course, Douglass had possessed no voice at all in mainstream society. In good measure his narrative is the story of how he achieved his distinctive and powerful voice.

The Brother, like Douglass, is denied a voice. Despite his silence, though, he is eloquent. Like Douglass and like Jim, he cannot use his name for fear of detection because, again like Douglass and like Jim, he is running from slave-catchers. To make the parallels with classic slave narrative absolutely clear in the reader's mind, the movie includes a sequence in which The Brother and a young boy (the son of his white landlady and her black lover) visit a museum. The Brother points to a picture of a fleeing slave and then to himself, repeatedly, a muted way of explaining to the child that he is a fugitive *just like* the slave in the picture. Additionally, the movie makes exuberant use of an illuminating visual pun in which the underground railroad of American history and the subway system of New York become the same thing.

The A-Train, which travels the movie's underground railroad, is The Brother's vehicle to freedom and safety. And although the A-Train goes *to* Harlem, it also goes *from* Harlem to other destinations, should anyone choose to ride it. There is a fairly early sequence in the movie in which a young white man (Fisher Stevens) identified in the credits as "card trickster" offers to show The Brother a trick as they ride. The trick is to make every white person get off the train—and sure enough they do. What The Brother does not know at the time is that the train has just arrived at the crucial station marking the boundary of Harlem. One thing that he learns is that he is far more likely to journey into white America than whites are to journey into black America.

A deeply effective and resonant symbol, the A-Train (and by extension the subway system) carries more than one meaning. It is not only the underground railroad but also an entryway to the underworld, which is itself a metaphor for the black man's urban home. The poetic night sequence, which includes a guide named Virgil, takes The Brother on a dark tour of his new home, showing him the vista of a city in the grip of its own nightmares. On this tour, The Brother seems able only to process images to which he is directed by Virgil. The reference to Dante Alighieri's *Commedia* is unmistakable, although the movie's Virgil is not exactly the poet referred to in Dante's *Inferno*. A brother who speaks with a Caribbean lilt, the movie's Virgil has an ironic quality that is both charming and frightening.

In the contemporary inferno revealed to The Brother, he sees the same street people that he sees by day. The difference is that without the reassuring glare of daylight their depravity and desolation are so extreme as to cause The Brother great anguish and to supply him a sense of mission. Having found a young man dead from a heroin overdose, he tries the drug himself in an effort to understand what has happened. He will subsequently declare his own war on drug traffic.

One effect of the city-after-dark nightmare sequence is to demonstrate how little life has improved for at least some of the descendants of American slaves, though this is hardly secret knowledge to anyone except The Brother. Another effect is to provide The Brother with a motive that can supersede his own escape, a cause to which he can dedicate himself without self-interest, sublimating concern with his own escape and survival to a larger cause, the liberation of others. The anti-drug theme that underlies this effort is parallel in some measure to the classic slave narrator's dedication to the abolitionist cause.[3] To liberate the young people of his

---

[3]Despite his dedication to the cause of Abolitionism, Douglass was practical in his consideration of his own freedom. At one point in his career as a speaker and fund raiser, friends of Douglass have raised money to purchase his freedom. On principle, William Lloyd Garrison advised against the purchase, believing that it was an admission of the right of ownership. Douglass felt, quite sensibly, that such an abstract point had to take a back seat to the concrete matter of securing his legal freedom from repossession.

new home from their enslavement to drugs is certainly an effort to secure them freedom, though not from literal owners.

There are differences between The Brother and an abolitionist such as Frederick Douglass, however. One difference is that in Sayles' movie, The Brother can engage in violence against his enemies without alienating his audience—a luxury not shared by writers like Frederick Douglass or by characters like Jim who could not engage in violence against whites (even those designated as "bad") without risking the deep alienation of a ("good") white audience whose support they required. Another equally telling difference is that The Brother may indulge in flirtation and sexual dalliance, activities well outside the range of the fugitive slave in the nineteenth century.

Very obviously, this movie offers a meditation on issues including racial prejudice and drug addiction. Less obviously, but no less effectively, it works as a meditation on the meanings of silence and the relationship between vision and power as all of these relate to social and economic position in American Society. In order to do this, *The Brother* draws on both literature and film.

For American slaves and the descendants of American slaves, silence (literally as well as metaphorically) has been a defining quality of life simply because African American culture and its expression were largely excluded from recognition by the dominant white culture. One consequence of this is the clear identification of power with voice—the understanding that if one is denied voice, one is denied power. At the same time, in The Brother's case, silence allows people to find in him what they need to find. Because *he* is silent, they can be whatever they wish to be with him, and can perceive in him whatever they project onto him. Denied verbal expression, The Brother allows people to read him as they will.

In addition to using the narrative format of the slave narrative, Sayles employs in the movie a generic convention of science fiction. *The Brother from Another Planet* uses the viewpoint of an alien to show the audience its own society, its own world. Put another way, the movie is about society here and now, and about the earthly humans of which that society is made up. The alien and his point of view, it is made clear, represent the historical outsider with an outsider's point of view as regards American culture and society.

The alien protagonist (Joe Morton), is stranded in America when his spaceship crashes on Ellis Island,[4] the now abandoned center for processing immigrants to the United States. This is so heavy handedly apt an arrival point that a viewer can hardly miss its significance. Although "reading" the location is not a problem for the audience, it is for the new arrival. At this point the we are introduced to one of his special abilities; the alien can hear the voices of the past. In the empty, echoing vault of the Ellis Island Reception Center, he hears a rising clamor of voices in a polyphony of languages.

As the scene develops, these voices seem to be as unintelligible to the alien as they are to most of the viewers—a babel of sound carrying the weight of emotional distress that The Brother himself might be expected to feel. What the audience must see, though the alien may not quite make the connection himself, is that the alien is only the most recent immigrant to arrive at Ellis Island. What his reception will be in the greater body of America is another question. People of color, historically, have not fared well there.

Because he has landed on an island, The Brother must cross water to get to his destination. One implication is that this crossing will mark a rebirth for the voyager in much the same way that his raft journey down the Mississippi marks a rebirth for Huck Finn. Another equally viable interpretation is that like a voyager crossing the River Styx, this particular traveler is about to descend into the underworld. This second view, lent some weight by the Virgil sequence, is not given

---

[4]In Twain's novel, Huck and Jim meet on Jackson's Island. Since an island is by definition cut off from land, surrounded by water, we begin very early to perceive in Huck and Jim a unit cut off from the surrounding culture and civilization that Huck will ultimately repudiate. In Sayles' movie, as The Brother comes to Ellis Island, and then Manhattan Island, alone, and the viewer is quick to perceive the extent of his isolation.

the same weight in the film's development as the first, but resonates beneath the film's dominant narrative line of flight to freedom.

As a newcomer to the United States, the Brother carries with him certain obvious handicaps. He is mute. He is deformed by terrestrial standards in that his feet have only three large toes instead of the five much smaller digits earthlings have come to expect. He is, to all appearances, a black man. This, in practical terms, is a handicap as well, perhaps the most serious of all, and is one that he shares with slave narrator Frederick Douglass.

In addition to his handicaps, all of which appear to be socially constructed, the Brother has certain gifts. We learn that he can regrow his own severed limbs. He can heal machines with a laying on of hands. He is supremely adaptable. He has skills that the residents of Harlem do not share. That he can survive a new and generally hostile environment with these attributes is remarkable. There is also the curious business of his eye—an organ which he can remove from his head and set up to view events when he must be absent. Like a miniature camcorder, this eye will replay for The Brother the events he was unable to view in person.

That The Brother can see the environment around him with shocking clarity, of course, is one of the major points of Sayles' movie. As alien, as outsider, he has none of the cultural filters that will prevent him from seeing accurately and objectively the situation in which he is placed. We (the audience) have already begun to see through alien eyes, already begun to align ourselves with The Brother's point of view in the developing narrative. As a sympathetic character moving continuously through the story, he is a powerful vehicle for audience identification. At one point, The Brother removes one of his eyes and leaves it in a sidewalk flower pot as a recording device. When he returns, the audience sees *with him* the scenes his eye has witnessed. When he views the events his eye has recorded, The Brother shares with us an objective experience, objective observation. Thus, Sayles presses the metaphor of seeing through another's eyes, visually literalizing it for the viewer.

It is both humorous and appropriate that the world The Brother comes to is the world of Harlem, with its liveliness, its hipness, its poverty, and its acute awareness of color. The Brother is not only black but he sports dreadlocks. By most American standards of dress, his clothing is peculiar but in the world of New York Harbor and then of Harlem, the same could be said of much of the visible population. His feet are effectively concealed by shoes. The Brother fits in. People help him out and he helps them out. But the story is a little more complicated because the alien is being pursued by two Men in Black, the legal agents who want to return him to slavery in the world that he has escaped.

As part of the film's commentary on color, these agents (David Strathairn and John Sayles) are white, a fact that seems to escape their notice, just as The Brother's blackness does. What makes them part of the power elite, apparently, is that they have five toes rather than three. And they have voices. The attributes of whiteness and voice might, in other terrestrial surrounds, have made it easier for these interstellar agents (perhaps, as Jerry Roberts suggests, bounty hunters {7} or perhaps, as The Brother has told us in all but words, slave catchers) to fit in. Yet in Harlem both work to their disadvantage. Being white makes them objects of amusement and suspicion. They are unable (as they work from what must be interplanetary Berlitz guides) to get anything right if it involves verbal expression, and proceed to order beer on the rocks (*The Brother from Another Planet*). Their ineptitude combines with their failure to perceive their own strangeness in this new place to prevent them from achieving their goal. They are unable to capture The Brother without alerting the local population which then mobilizes successfully in his defense.

The alien—with all his strangeness—has become the lens of the film maker at the same time he has become the organ of vision for the audience. All of this suggests a certain "inside-outness" to the operation of the film, a quality that John Sayles as auteur shares with Samuel Clemens as author. It is difficult not to discuss Sayles in terms of auteur theory as the individual "primarily responsible for the entire style and treatment of the content of a film" (Bywater 222), simply because the category fits him so well. My concern here, however, is somewhat more local. As writer/director,

Sayles *is* responsible for a great deal. As actor he also makes a contribution.

In this essay, I have been led in large part by the issue of textual appropriation as it manifests itself in Twain's most celebrated novel and again, a scant hundred years later, in John Sayles' film. Where Twain wrenches the slave narrative into the context of Huck's perceptions, Sayles displaces it into contemporary Harlem, which serves as an underground railroad station on an interplanetary underground railroad. It seems to me, as I consider these two works, that both authors reveal varying degrees of awareness and discomfort with a story they feel compelled to (choose your own word here) retell, exploit, or recreate. I suggest that this awareness and discomfort with their respective narrative properties is revealed in the repeated doubling of characters and author within the two works, both of which stand as cultural texts in which white men are encoding for a largely white audience the story of a black man's anguish and triumph.

The business of doubling, in Twain's work, occurs on two levels. First, we see a doubling within the novel, in which Huck and Jim become different sides of the heroic character—one brave, whimsical, antic—and the other mature, seasoned, quiet. One, not coincidentally, is white while the other is black.[5] These two "joined" or "doubled" heroes do not always fully understand each other. Yet there is a tremendous body of shared experience that pulls them together. Both are from social underclasses and thus may be predisposed to some degree of sympathy with one another. In their journey down the river they share the same raft, eat the same food, meet the same characters, and form remarkably similar judgements of them.

Another doubling of character (though not fully explored in *The Adventures of Huckleberry Finn*) occurs with Huck and Tom Sawyer, who seem to represent what might be two essential aspects of boyhood and, outside of the question of age, of the American character as it is shaped by class. Both Huck and Tom are mischievous, both male, both restless in school. Otherwise, they are different in ways

---

[5]For a fuller discussion of this doubled hero, see "Seeing in Black and White: Suppressed Racial Violence . . ."

that reflect social class more than any other factor. Tom comes from the middle class haven of Aunt Polly's house[6] where, among other things, he has apparently learned how to read and found great joy in the accomplishment. His entire imagination is shaped by the reading of action adventures rich in pirate loot and spiked with a great deal of swashbuckling behavior.

Huck, by contrast, comes from no home at all, since his drunken father cannot be said to provide one. Unlike Tom, Huck is a stranger to well-made clothes and can scarcely abide shoes. He does not understand, as Tom does, that in society a certain degree of decorum is necessary and that this decorum is frequently supplied by the practice of duplicity. He lacks Tom's more "civilized" instinct for acceptable behavior. Huck's own instincts, though morally laudable by the end of his adventures with Jim, are the product of practical experience and observation. In short, Tom is a distinctly middle-class literary figure while Huck is an at best semi-literate son of the working class.

A rather intriguing question in this peculiarly American brew is just where the reader might expect to find author Samuel Clemens—or is it Mark Twain? Van Wyck Brooks suggested as long ago as 1920 that Clemens himself was tormented by his desire to be free of social convention and its hypocrisy and his equally strong desire for acceptance and approval within that very society. It is, rather obviously, the case that the author "doubles" himself in pretty significant fashion. He 'lives' under one name, writes under another. In 'real life,' particularly in later life, he is subject to all sorts of emotional distress as well as to the carbuncle-like indignities of aging that come to most of humankind; in the 'writing life' he is by turns sentimental and acidic but is always the ironist. He is, then, not a simple figure to unravel. Nor is his text on Huck Finn made simpler if we go hunting for its author in its pages. For the sake of convenience and out of a fondness for puns, I'll refer to the author as "Twain"

---

[6]As with Huck Finn after his adoption by the Widder Douglass, this adolescent male is reared exclusively by women, a circumstance that aligns civilization with feminization.

(two) henceforth. In *The Adventures of Huckleberry Finn* "doubling" is a technique that offers some hints as to where Twain himself is at various points.

It is not difficult to read Twain reflecting himself in the characters he has created. To some extent, he seems to be reflected in Jim, whose fugitive status keeps him as nearly invisible as he can manage. This invisibility is somewhat suggestive of the "invisible" presence in the text of the author, with whom Jim shares a more profound understanding of the complex demands of American life than Huck Finn himself has yet achieved.

At the same time, Twain is "doubling" as both Huckleberry Finn and Tom Sawyer. Tom Sawyer, in his exuberant desire to turn every event into an adventure yarn, represents a peculiarly literary turn of mind in which Twain himself participates in real life. Twain is, after all, taking the story of a runaway slave and turning it into a different adventure—coming of age. The moral problem with Tom Sawyer, both as a hero and as a reflection of his author, is that he is, morally, irremediably obtuse. He is consumed by the glamor of his reading life to the exclusion of any useful judgement of life as it must be lived by real, everyday human beings.

Twain is reflected equally clearly in Huck, who shares with the author a deep love for the river and an equally deep sense of the hypocrisies of civilization. Huck, unlike Tom Sawyer, is capable of moral growth and genuine outrage in the face of injustice, both of which are qualities we as readers attribute to Twain because he has so skillfully enlisted our sympathies on Huck's behalf. Unfortunately, Huck does not sustain this courageous stance.

By the close of *The Adventures of Huckleberry Finn*, Jim is in a very bad spot. He has been captured and confined. The rational expectation is that he will be returned to a life of continuing slavery or else sold away from his family. In an incredible bit of coincidence even for fiction, Tom Sawyer arrives to visit the family which now has possession of Jim. He recognizes but does not betray his friend Huck. When told of Jim's predicament, he enthusiastically sets about engineering an escape which, modeled on Tom's literary excursions, brings both humiliation and injury to

Jim and is ultimately foiled.

None of this could occur without Huck's acquiescence. Tom has actually brought Jim word of his freedom, but withholds news of Jim's manumission as long as he can. Why? Because to Tom, everything is a game with a literary flavor. In this, of course, he is irresponsible. Huck, who eschews civilization for "the territories," is also irresponsible. If both can be excused because they are, after all, only boys, then the novel becomes a treacherous tale that endorses the abuse of the principles Huck seems to have allied himself with. Tom's moral sense, if he has one, is still unformed.

Not so Huck's. He has denounced racial prejudice and the hypocritical demands of "womanish" civilization. He abandons the world that made both him and Jim, and Tom as well, for the promise offered by new territories. This is, on the surface, laudable. But he abandons as well those who are part of his deepest self—Jim and Tom. His irresponsibility seems cleaner than Tom's because of Huck so strongly desires a locus thus far undefiled by the very civilization that has already corrupted America nearly beyond redemption. Huck himself, in a powerful irony, will inevitably become part of the corrupting (and imperialistic) force from which he runs.

The novel is, in short, both a good and a guilty narrative: good in that it enlists its readers on the side of justice, revealing the hideous mistreatment of the African American under slavery and guilty in that it lets art (both the literary Tom Sawyer and the novel itself) off the hook by having the darker son of America (Jim) step aside voluntarily, returning to his family and thereby surrendering the vast promise of the new territories to a white boy who has already failed him at least once. In Twain's case, I suspect, there is a lurking suspicion of the irrelevance of the novel, an undertow of feeling that a real hero would not write such a book, but fight for justice in the nation's social and political trenches.

Regarding John Sayles and *The Brother from Another Planet*, all this raises a similar question—is Sayles inside the film or outside it? We can easily say that as writer he is *outside*. He is the creator of a script that is the product of his imagination, his vision, his desire to project something onto the cinema screen. As director, to a great extent, he must still be defined as *outside*. He is now the one who interprets the writer's script for actors and crew in order to best represent the writer's work. So as writer and director, working from an intellectual position outside the script, Sayles exercises a nearly absolute power over what finally appears on screen. In this, he is comparable to the author of a book. Twain, for example, clearly occupies a position *outside* of his novel (*Huckleberry Finn*). The book, whatever the sources of its material and structure, is the product of the writer's imagination and arrangement of words.

Yet it is also true that, just as Twain also exists inside the novel, Sayles is rather paradoxically *inside* the film, understanding it from creative perspectives that are unlikely to be shared fully by members of the cast and crew who are, finally, working under his direction and not independently. The role Sayles takes as an actor can be read as a metaphor for this position .

As one of the Men in Black, he exercises great authority. He is emphatically *not* part of the community that has welcomed The Brother. As a Man in Black, he is also not part of the city bureaucracy he attempts to tap. He cannot make himself readily understood by use of words, a difficulty he shares, ironically, with The Brother. Yet he is, very obviously, *The Man*. He is a threat. He controls. He must be appeased or outwitted in some way if The Brother, who is the film's hero, is to survive.

The Men in Black (who bear an uncanny resemblance to birds of prey) make excellent thematic foils for The Brother Himself. They are his doubles in their alienness and unfamiliarity with the territory they explore, and although they can speak, the language of Harlem is closed to them. But they are not like The Brother in any fundamental sense. Where their misuse of language sets them apart, The Brother's silence allows him to become part of the community. The Men in Black are also The Brother's opposites in color, status, and the way they react to the life forms they find on planet earth. Where The Brother is curious and friendly, the Men in Black are demanding and threatening. Where The Brother is self-effacing, no threat to the people of the community, the Men in Black are an active threat to The Brother and those who give him shelter. Where The Brother is courageous, the Men in Black are cowardly bullies.   At the same time, the Men in Black can be seen as effective doubles for the writer/director who is giving shape to the film. Like the Men in Black, the writer/director is at the very heart of things. It is his vision, his sense of order, that make the plot move. Like the Men in Black, he must also be the outsider, the alien, who attempts to see the entire picture at once.   In this respect, the writer/director is not unlike The Brother himself. Both represent an area of silence in which the cast and crew develop and explore their own interpretations and strategies as the film comes into being. The Brother, as he finds something like his own place in Harlem, is a clear example of the power of such silence.

The Brother can be compared to the character of Chance (Peter Sellers), a retarded man employed as a gardener in Hal Ashby's 1980 film, *Being There*. Though not mute, Chance is prevented by his disability from being able to communicate. In effect, he is denied a voice. Although the similarities of the two lie on the surface of their characters, the responses to them of other characters are informative. Because Chance is exceedingly passive and The Brother is mute, both characters are interpreted by others in terms of their own perceptions. Because he does not speak, The Brother (like Chance) becomes a sort of tabula rasa for those who help him.   None of them divine his real story, a fact that adds considerable piquancy for the viewer.[7]

If his silence gives The Brother some of the same receptivity exhibited by Chance, his own nature gives him a far more active role in determining his fate. Where Chance rises to a position of power because others put him there, The Brother puts

---

[7]The Brother's muteness has also led to broadly divergent characterizations of the script: for the unnamed writer of the *Biography* on the Internet's *John Sayles Border Stop*, "the film relies on brilliant performances from a tightly knit cast to bring to life a talk-heavy script." For Leonard Maltin, it is "full of fine dialog" (1) Like the characters who invent their own versions of The Brother, the critics seem to invent their own versions of the movie.

himself into most of the situations we are shown and acts in his own best interest. Where Chance is a passive figure to whom things happen, The Brother is actively engaged in pursuit of his own freedom and is willing to oppose evil with violence. Unlike Chance, The Brother is possessed of a keen intelligence to match his emotional sensitivity. *Being There* presents the audience with "an empty vessel who rises to command" (Thomson 683); *The Brother From Another Planet* presents a hero who is, albeit quietly, vigorously shaping his own destiny. Where Chance acquiesces to events, The Brother anticipates and reacts to them.

It would be easy to apply to The Brother a description like the one David Thomson awards John Sayles, of whom he writes as ". . . himself a mass of men . . . . an odd droll actor . . . altogether earnest, likeable, hardworking. . ." (666-7) Thomson continues, " Indeed, for all his variety, there is an emphatic integrity to Sayles . . . as if he lacked the imagination for betrayal. (666-7)[8] Yet obviously, if the double presences in the film are to have meaning, betrayal is not a concept Sayles has ignored. Sayles himself exists both inside and outside the film. By taking an actor's role as a Man in Black, one of the interstellar cops or slave catchers in pursuit of the Brother, he acknowledges the peculiar position he must occupy as a white man telling a black man's story.

The double presence (or presence of doubles) in *The Brother from Another Planet* is amplified by two white characters—friends from out-of-town who are in the city for a self-actualization seminar at Columbia. They are, to employ a popular and

---

[6]Sayles, in *The Brother From Another Planet,* is working on what Thomson identifies as "a crowded canvas" (667)—a canvas virtually cluttered with characters and plots and complications. This has led some to dismiss the work, as David Thomson does, as "painfully awkward" (667). Others, like Leonard Maltin, believe that the movie overextends itself with the segments of plot in which The Brother takes on the drug issue, accompanying the firelit figure of Virgil through Harlem's nighttime streets and finally killing the white rising yuppie executive who is the brain behind a drug distribution network, but that it is ultimately worth watching anyway. While the Virgil segment of the movie slows the pace considerably, it seems unfair to condemn the movie for including it.

useful expression, absolutely clueless about Harlem and about African Americans. White and middle-class, they are (geographically as well as socially and emotionally) totally lost as they search for Columbia University. They are acutely aware that they have no business being in the neighborhood in which they find themselves. In this respect, they too are rather like Sayles, who has invaded a narrative territory to which, as a white man, his claim is in some respects dubious. Like Twain's novel, the film enlists the reader on the side of justice, and like Twain's novel, it is aware of the license it takes in order to do so.

What is perhaps most important, and so obvious that it may be difficult to see, is that both *The Adventures of Huckleberry Finn* and *The Brother from Another Planet* are appropriated narratives, stories to which the authors, one assumes, have right because of their ability to shape narrative, because of the power of their imaginations. Yet the slave narrative remains, culturally and literally, the first person narrative of a human being escaping from chattel slavery into freedom. Huck's narrative is Jim's story recast as the tale of a white boy coming of age in an America so young it has yet to fight the Civil War. The Brother's story is also the narrative of a black man's escape from slavery, told this time by a white male adult who is writer, director, and even actor.

That Sayles goes ahead and appropriates the narrative at all suggests that as a culture we are still enmeshed in the problem of good and guilty narratives in much the same way that Twain was. On one hand, we seem not to have come terribly far in the past one hundred and thirty something years. The black man is still largely muted, still pursued by retributive forces when he seeks freedom, and demonstrably owes survival to the strength of the black community. On the other hand, given the ways in which Sayles uses his film to comment on the irony of his authorial stance, we may be moving ahead at a surprisingly smart pace.

46

Works Cited

Being There. Dir. Hal Ashby. With Peter Sellers, Shirley MacLaine. Lorimar. 1980.

"Biography." *The John Sayles Border Stop.* Http://www-scf.usc.edu~/bio/bio.html.
  Accessed 1/7/98.

Bywater, Tim and Thomas Sobchak. *Introduction to Film Criticism: Major Critical*
  Approaches to Narrative Film. NY: Longman, 1989.

Douglass, Frederick. *The Narrative and Selected Writings.* Ed. Michael Meyer. NY:
  Random House (Modern Library Ed.), 1984.

Graff, Gerald and James Phelan. *A Case Study in Critical Controversy: Adventures of*
  Huckleberry Finn. NY: Bedford/St. Martin's, 1995.

Maltin, Leonard. *"The Brother From Another Planet." Leonard Maltin's Movie &*
  Video Guide. Http://cinemania.msn.com/Movie/MaltinReview/2135.

Marx, Leo. "Mr. Eliot, Mr. Trilling, and *Huckleberry Finn.*" Graff & Phelan. 290-305.

Meyer, Michael. "Introduction." Douglass. i-xxxii.

Olney, James. *Autobiography: Essays Theoretical & Critical.* Princeton: Princeton
  UP, 1980.

Olney, James. "Autobiography & the Cultural Moment." In Olney. 3-27.

Roberts, Jerry. "True Indie: The films of John Sayles." ©1996.
  Http://cinemania.msn.com/VideoRewind/Artifle/13. Accessed 1/7/98.

Rosenblatt, Roger. "Black Autobiography: Life as Death Weapon." Olney.169-80.

The Brother from Another Planet. Dir. John Sayles. With Joe Morton, David
  Strathairn, John Sayles. A-Train Films. 1984.

Sayre, Robert F. "Autobiography and the Making of America." Olney. 146-168.

Thomson, David. *A Biographical Dictionary of Film. Third Edition.* NY: Alfred
  Knopf, Inc. 1994.

Twain, Mark. *The Adventures of Huckleberry Finn.* Graff & Phelan. 27-265.

"History with Lightning":[1]
The Legacy of D.W. Griffith's *The Birth of a Nation*

We do not fear censorship . . .

—*Title Card*
The Birth of a Nation

Released in 1915, D.W. Griffith's groundbreaking epic, *The Birth of a Nation*, represents a noteworthy moment in the history of American film. The movie is generally admitted to have set the narrative and technical standards for the film industry. It is also generally admitted to have reflected and capitalized upon the worse than uneasy racial climate of the country. Even today, *The Birth of a Nation* is a remarkably powerful and controversial document of American popular culture.

The substance of this nearly three hour extravaganza, drawn largely from Thomas Dixon's anti-black novel *The Clansman*, consists of a pair of love stories, a melodrama of post Civil War Reconstruction, and the crucial fable of the white race's return to power and union through the leadership of the Ku Klux Klan. The love stories provide for the romantic union of the white children of North and South. The melodrama of Reconstruction presents white Southerners of the planter class assaulted and humiliated by arrogant, foolish, and bullying blacks. The fable of the

---

[1]This is part of Woodrow Wilson's description of *The Birth of a Nation* after its White House screening. "It is like writing history with lightning" (Mast and Kawn 66; Franklin 46).

Ku Klux Klan presents that organization as the only saving and unifying force in a nation beleaguered by rebellious and vengeful former slaves.

Like most of Griffith's work, *The Birth of a Nation* is plagued by his weaknesses as a director and story teller. The characters are one dimensional and artificial. The plots are thin and obviously contrived. The story relies heavily on the use of didactic title cards and superimposed allegorical figures (Mast & Kawn 63) to direct the audience's thinking. Nonetheless, the movie retains a great deal of its power because of the skill with which the director intertwines plots and because of the innovative and masterful cinematic techniques he employs. With a running time of 165 minutes (subsequent to a nine minute cut), *The Birth of a Nation* became the longest and most ambitious film of its day.

In addition to other innovations, *The Birth of a Nation* makes more extensive and skillful use of crosscutting than had previously been seen. Griffith cuts not only between parallel stories, but between stories and title cards,[2] and (most originally) between the broad action of a story line and closeups of the individual characters involved. This serves to generate tension and suspense as well as to create nuance and depth of expression. The imposition of allegorical figures, as at the movie's close when the horseman of war is replaced by a dissolve into the prince of peace, may appear clumsy and overstated by today's standards but in 1915 was stunning in effect.

No summary can do full justice to three hours of film interweaving multiple plots and a large cast of characters. Nonetheless, some overview of the stories in the movie is necessary to a discussion of its significance and effects. The movie is presented in two parts, the first of which deals with events leading to Reconstruction (primarily with the Civil War), and the second with Reconstruction itself. The

---

[2]Admittedly, title cards were a hallmark of silent movies. Under Griffith's direction, however, they served to heighten the drama of a sequence in the same way that drama is heightened by cross cutting to a clock's hands while a condemned prisoner waits for a last minute pardon. For a particularly effective example of this, one has only to watch the assassination of Abraham Lincoln as presented in *The Birth of a Nation.*

characters (whose lives demonstrate the rightness of the movie's racial and political perspective) occupy both historical periods.

The parallel love stories involve two white American families, the Stonemans from the North and the Camerons from the South. These families represent the "real" (read "white") America. The Northern patriarch is Congressman Austin Stoneman (Ralph Lewis), modeled with great (one is tempted to say libelous) liberty[3] on the historical figure of Thaddeus Stevens. Stoneman is a liberal and thus a "bad" white man[4]. Devoted to the political and social advancement of African Americans, he cannot master his lust for Lydia Brown (Mary Alden), his opportunistic mulatto housekeeper. Of his two sons, the younger, Tod (Robert Harron), will die in the Civil War, ironically reunited with one of the Cameron sons who also dies. The elder Stoneman son, Phil (Elmer Clifton), will survive and marry Margaret Cameron (Miriam Cooper), a true daughter of the South. Austin Stoneman's one daughter is the beautiful Elsie (Lillian Gish).

The Southern patriarch, Dr. Cameron (Aitkin Spottiswoode), is a wealthy planter who lives with his wife and children in a mansion located in fictional Piedmont, South Carolina. If Cameron is the model patriarch, his wife (Josephine Crowell) is the model Southern mistress of the planter class, a courteous, subdued matron who dotes upon her children. The Cameron's children include their eldest son, Ben (Henry B.Walthall) and his two younger brothers, Wade (George Beranger) and Duke (Maxfield Stanley). Like Tod Stoneman these two younger sons will die in the Civil War. The Camerons also boast two daughters, of whom the elder, Margaret, ultimately to marry Phil Stoneman, is described as "a daughter of the old South

---

[3]Although Dixon publically declared that he had revealed the real Thaddeus Stevens, the real Stevens was a childless bachelor, never went to South Carolina, and so far as is known, did not conduct an affair with his black housekeeper (Franklin 49).

[4]It is the vengeful Stoneman who says to Lincoln, after Appomattox, that the Southerners' "leaders must be hanged and their states treated as conquered provinces" (*The Birth of a Nation*).

trained in manners of the old school" (*The Birth of a Nation*). Her sister Flora (Mae Marsh), the youngest of the Cameron children, who leaps to her death to escape the advances of a former slave, is described as "Flora, the little pet sister"(*The Birth of a Nation*). Cameron's wealth, derived from the work of his many slaves, allows his family to live in mythic comfort and gentility within the plantation system of the old south.

As the stories of these northern and southern families develop and interconnect, the audience sees the older sons as school friends and the younger sons as chums. Later, of course, they will meet as adversaries on the battle field where the younger sons die. The elder sons each fall in love with the beautiful daughter of the other family. These burgeoning love stories are nearly derailed by the Civil War, Emancipation, and Reconstruction. All obstacles are finally overcome, however, and both couples are united—a symbolic double marriage of the white north and the white south.

If the young people of the Stoneman and Cameron families appear as victims of the war, the same cannot be said of the major figures in the Reconstruction melodrama. In this plot, the audience is given two primary villains, the senior Stoneman and his mulatto henchman Silas Lynch (George Siegmann), who is appointed by Stoneman to be Lieutenant Governor of South Carolina. The plot is developed in a pastiche of scenes in which the old master (Cameron) is tormented by his former slaves whose freedom affords them the chance to abuse the man who has, if the film is to be taken seriously, cared well for them in the past. Cameron is ultimately rescued by the "good" black, the family's mammy, who is identified in the film's cast list as "Mammy, *the faithful servant*" (*The Birth of a Nation*).

An even more provocative subplot is developed in which Gus (Walter Long), "a renegade negro" (*The Birth of a Nation*) makes advances to Flora Cameron. To escape him,[5] she leaps from a high cliff to her death. Meanwhile, Silas Lynch is

---

[5]In the novel, Gus's crime is rape. In the movie, Flora's terror is sparked by Gus's unlikely statement, "You see, I'm a Captain now–and I want to marry" (*The Birth of*

pursuing Elsie Stoneman. Miscegenation, clearly, is perceived by the film's makers as a serious threat and an absolute evil.

The saga of the birth and rise of the Ku Klux Klan, introduced well into the movie's second part, is necessary both to draw the preceding plots together and to establish for the audience the heroic nature of the Klan itself. This heroic nature arises from what the movie presents as the inherent necessity for and the indisputable rightness of white rule. These notions are underscored by the emergence of the Klan, which the movie links by implication to such pious phrases as "out of the mouths of babes . . ." and "a little child shall lead them."

Ben Cameron has returned home from the war. He is recovered from his physical though not his emotional wounds, which include the loss of his family's wealth, the deaths of his brothers, and the loss of political power by white South Carolinians. He sits on a mountainside agonizing "over the degradation and ruin of his people" (*The Birth of a Nation*). A pair of white children come up the path, carrying with them a white sheet or blanket. They spy a group of four black children further down the trail and hide under their sheet to wait. When the black children arrive, the white children, draped in the white sheet, begin making scary noises, swaying like a misshapen ghost. The black children run away terrified and Ben Cameron is stricken with inspiration. Thus, according to the movie, the KKK is born.[6]

Subsequently, the Klan is shown throwing the fear of God into fractious blacks and avenges the implied violation of Flora Cameron by capturing and executing

---

a Nation). The rape is implicit in the racist view of blacks that the film projects, and the audience is told by the following title card that "we should not grieve that she found sweeter the opal gates of death" (*The Birth of a Nation*).

[6]Nothing in my reading supports this version of the Ku Klux Klan's origins. In fact, the Klan was born in Tennessee in 1866, not on a mountainside in South Carolina. That this sequence takes for granted a stereotypical perception of blacks as childish and credulous both derives from and supports the use of stereotypical figures in the plantation genre.

Gus.[7] When his dead body is delivered to Silas Lynch, bearing a note that says KKK, the accompanying title card bears the caption: "The answer to blacks and scalawags" (*The Birth of a Nation*). Thus the Ku Klux Klan makes the world, or at least this particular part of the South, safe once more for whites, whose rule is the only way the movie allows for the nation to achieve stability underpinned by sound moral and ethical values.

Within the film industry, the influence of *The Birth of a Nation* has been extensive, particularly in technical innovation and narrative technique. According to Elliott Carter, the movie does indeed herald a birth, but not "of a nation." Rather it is the birth "of an American industry and an American art; any attempt to define the cinema and its impact upon American life must take into account this classic movie" (Carter 9).

With *The Birth of a Nation*, the plantation tradition in film makes a monumental and highly influential appearance. In this tradition, at least until the release of *Gone With the Wind*,[8] the Civil War remains the War of Northern Aggression; the Southern plantation is presented as an Edenic site in which slaves and their owners live harmoniously and happily. White Southern womanhood, as a rule, is genteel, lovely, and humane. White Southern men tend to be dashing cavaliers. Anomalous figures (a Jezebel, a Scarlett O'Hara) serve to underscore the rightness

---

[7]Before embarking on its mission to find Gus, the Klan observes a ritual dipping of the flag in the blood of the dead and dishonored Flora Cameron, surely a noteworthy ceremony for these self proclaimed Christian knights.

[8]As pointed out by film historian Ed Guerrero, *The Birth of Nation* exists for African Americans as the "starkly racist slander of 1915" (3). It was not until the middle 1970's that Hollywood productions underwent a shift of perspective in the plantation genre, with such movies as *Drum* (1975, Dino de Laurentiis Productions) and *Mandingo*, (1976, Dino de Laurentiis Productions, Paramount Pictures). Both movies were lurid presentations of the plantation as a nightmarish locus of perverse sex and human abuse. There had been Hollywood challenges to at least some of the plantation steretypes in such earlier movies as *The Little Foxes* (RKO Pictures and Samuel Goldwyn Co., 1942) and *Pinky* (Twentieth Century Fox, 1949) but these were not full-fledged plantation dramas.

of the genteel, decorous social order represented by the white, aristocratic South. The slaves in this genre are represented generally as being both happy with their lot and endlessly loyal to their owners. To be sure, there are some flawed (rebellious) blacks, but they serve, like the anomalous white characters, to underscore the Edenic nature of the Southern plantation.

Drawing heavily on the already established literary tradition of plantation fiction, the plantation tradition in film generally and in *The Birth of a Nation* in particular offer numerous stereotypes that support the racist agenda of the genre. Within the "Southern" point of view espoused by both D.W. Griffith and Thomas Dixon, who share writing credit for the movie, there are good whites (like the Camerons) and bad whites (like Congressman Stoneman).

The good whites are Southerners—Christian, chaste, genteel, devoted to and supported by the subjugation of blacks in America. They have larger families and deeper loyalties than Yankees. They are good looking, as the patriarchal Dr. Cameron demonstrates. "The kindly master of Cameron Hall" (*The Birth of a Nation*), no longer young, is tall and dignified, sporting a mane of silvering hair and even features. The bad whites in the movie's America are Northerners—political liberals, victims of their own lust, easily manipulated by opportunistic (bad) blacks. They are not physically attractive. Congressman Stoneman, for instance, wears a bad wig and has a deformed foot that skews his gait—defects of the body that mirror defects of the soul. He is seduced by his mulatto housekeeper, a failing described in Griffith's title card as "The Great Leader's weakness that is to blight a nation" (*The Birth of a Nation*). In terms of race, white is still better than black, however, and the bad white may produce good offspring who can be salvaged by their Southern brothers and sisters.

Within the same perspective, there are good blacks and bad blacks. The good blacks are loyal servants who rejoice in their lot and will do anything to help their owners. Typical representatives are the mammy, a substantial figure who brooks no nonsense from less contented blacks and who both mothers and otherwise supports her "white family." Joining her in the gallery of black goodness are the loyal slave (exemplified by the field hands and house servants who do NOT repudiate their masters after Emancipation) and the dancing buck, a variant on the happy darky of plantation fiction. Like the mammy, who in *The Birth of a Nation* saves the now aged and frail Dr. Cameron (who is being tormented by a handful of former slaves), the happy darky is present on the Cameron plantation, represented by the host of field hands who while away their two hour dinner break (*The Birth of a Nation*) both for their own pleasure and for the entertainment of whites who happen by. The most telling traits of all good blacks are that they recognize their place in the scheme of things and believe they need white masters in order to prosper.

Mulattos form a subclass of blacks in *The Birth of a Nation*. Unlike other blacks, they are presented as being incapable of goodness. Stoneman's housekeeper, Lydia Brown, is an example of the mulatto woman who trades on the combination of her light skin and black sexuality to ensnare (or perhaps enslave) Congressman Stoneman. According to one of Griffith's title cards, she is "roused from ambitious dreamings by Sumner's curt orders" (*The Birth of a Nation*). She later trades on her status as Stoneman's paramour to insult Sumner, who (it is implied) is more discerning than Stoneman himself. Similarly, the mulatto Silas Lynch is in some way "spoiled" by his white blood, although this is not fully evident until he is given political control over the state of South Carolina, presumably a task beyond his scope. Believing that even though he remains "black" in the eyes of society, he is now entitled to "white" privilege, Lynch begins his pursuit of a white woman (Elsie Stoneman) who rejects his proposal of marriage and whom he kidnaps in order to secure her submission.

Gus, the "renegade Negro" (*The Birth of a Nation*) is not only a character whose villainy serves to advance the dramatic action of the movie. He allows the white characters to enact their fear of miscegenation. Gus is, given his desire to wed a white woman, the embodiment of an evil so terrifying to the movie's whites that they must destroy him—an act they perform with righteous enthusiasm under the aegis of the Klan.

Given certain general facts about American life in 1915, it is not surprising that the film's impending release generated a near firestorm of public response. The migration of southern blacks to the north had achieved great strength. The youthful NAACP, founded in 1910, was already working actively to promote full social equality for blacks in America and was to mount an important protest and boycott of Griffith's epic. At the same time, many whites in both the North and South subscribed to the belief that African Americans were inferior and had to be kept disenfranchised to the greatest extent possible—to be kept, in other words, in their place.

Among these whites were novelist Thomas Dixon and President Woodrow Wilson, whose *History of the American People* is quoted in some of the movie's more heavily textualized frames. In the course of the controversy surrounding its release, *The Birth of a Nation* became the first American film to be screened at the White House and the first to be screened for members of Congress and the Supreme Court. Without the cooperation of three white men—Dixon, Griffith, and Wilson—*The Birth of a Nation* might have had a somewhat different place in film history.

Thomas Dixon, today remembered chiefly for his connection with *The Birth of a Nation,* is a figure worth looking at. Born in 1864, Dixon spent his early years in the general vicinity of Shelby, North Carolina. At the age of eight, he would later claim, he witnessed a legislative session of the South Carolina state legislature comprised of "ninety-four Negroes, seven native scalawags, and twenty-three white men" (cited in Franklin 43) which he found so horrifying that its memory never left him.

A restless intelligence, Dixon was a graduate of Wake Forest College. He also spent some time at Johns Hopkins University. There he became a friend of Woodrow Wilson, who was at that time engaged in graduate work. At the age of 20, Dixon served a term in the North Carolina State Legislature (Franklin 43). Subsequently, he tried his hand as an essayist, an actor, a lawyer, a clergyman, and a lecturer

(Franklin 43). When he turned to literature, he secured the help of another school friend, Walter Hines Page of Doubleday, to secure publication. Dixon's purpose, throughout his career, was to inform the larger world of the "true" state of affairs in the South, and to discredit what he believed was the skewed Yankee version of events during the Civil War and Reconstruction periods.

Dixon's trio of novels about the Reconstruction Period (*The Leopard's Spots: A Romance of the White Man's Burden,* published in 1903; *The Clansman: An Historical Romance of the Ku Klux Klan,* published in 1905; and *The Traitor: A Story of the Rise and Fall of the Invisible Empire,* published in 1907) combined to give him credence as a Southern expert on the period—one whose direct experience underlay his work, although he would almost certainly have been too young during Reconstruction to have remembered the events he recounts, many of which did not even occur.

The most successful of his novels, *The Clansman,* Dixon recast as a play, seeking a broader audience for the Southern point of view (Franklin 44) regarding the Civil War, Reconstruction, and race. Ultimately, he came to believe that film was the greatest mover of the masses and an excellent vehicle for his material. He was extremely lucky in finding David Wark Griffith, a Kentuckian with some sympathy for Dixon's cultural perspective. Griffith had grasped the potential for increased scope in the cinema, and was very eager to make something larger and more ambitious than a one-reeler (Franklin 45). The film began to take shape. After six weeks of rehearsal, *The Birth of a Nation* began shooting on July 4, 1914 and took nine weeks to complete (Mast and Kawn 63).

Although the movie relies most heavily on *The Clansman* for its material, it also draws on the other novels to some extent. While some film analysts like Mast and Kawn (63) maintain that the film contains a good deal of Griffith,[9] especially in its

---

[9]Louis Gianetti and Scott Eyman maintain that "as a Southerner Griffith was actually something of a liberal—for his day. But he understood blacks only as a liberal nineteenth-century Southerner understood them: Negroes who were faithful . . . to

pre-war sequences, historian John Hope Franklin asserts that the movie's content is "pure Dixon" (Franklin 45). There are cases to be made for both viewpoints. Whichever case is more accurate, the movie itself remains a problematic cultural document. While the movie, as a racist fiction, may be objectionable, *The Birth of a Nation* is most troubling in its claim to be an accurate reconstruction of historical events. This claim is, quite simply, a lie.

As already established, the movie is riddled with racist assertions, both overt and implicit. In addition to the character stereotypes derived from plantation fiction, the movie's second title card holds the caption: "The bringing of the first African to America planted the first seed of disunion." Following this card is the image of cringing blacks moving from slave ship to sale block, passing before the raised praying arms and judgmental countenance of a New England Puritan. By implication this places the blame for the South's peculiar institution on the North, an assertion that contains some truth but that serves in the film as an exculpatory oversimplification.

Some time later in the film, as the young Stonemans and Camerons stroll about in idyllically rendered cotton fields, we are shown the slave quarters. Here "(i)n the two hour interval given for dinner out of their working day for six till six" (*The Birth of a Nation*) a host of well dressed slaves[10] dances with great energy for the amusement of their white visitors.

If blaming the presence of Africans in America for the Civil War and

---

their former masters were accorded respect and affection; blacks who were not loyalists were, by definition, slavering thugs with dangerous urges toward white women. Griffith's treatment of the race conflict and the Ku Klux Klan . . .to modern eyes, may appear insupportable. . . a measure of his restraint can be gauged by scanning his source material, an indescribably purple, extended rape fantasy whose author saw African-Americans as completely subhuman creatures who had to be either subjugated or exterminated" (32).

[10]The women wear respectable dresses and aprons; the men are in shirts and various sorts of pants. Here one can see one of the directorial "goofs" that bedevil most movies, as one of the dancing slaves is wearing the same spotted pants worn by a debarking African in the Puritan scene.

58

Reconstruction can be charitably viewed as oversimplification, the representation of slavery as a beneficent institution, full of happy, dancing field hands who live and dress as well as these, cannot. It is a misrepresentation of slavery as it existed in the real south—an idealization of a southern Eden into which the serpent came dressed as an African.

The proof of the African's nature, of course, is revealed in the consistent threat posed by blacks to whites during the movie's version of Reconstruction, a version flatly contradicted by reality.[11] Thus, for instance, there was no black lieutenant governor who corresponded to Silas Lynch and the vengeful behavior of freed South Carolinian slaves was entirely fictitious. For the most part, folks simply continued where they were, doing the jobs they were already doing in a different economic relation to their former owners.

The second part of the movie is introduced by a title card that avers: "This is an historical presentation of the Civil War and Reconstruction Periods . . ." (*The Birth of a Nation*). This announcement is followed by the following quotations from Woodrow Wilson's *History of the American People*. In this text, they are arranged as they appear, sequentially, on title cards in the movie.

> ¶ . . . . . Adventurers swarmed out of the North, as much the
> enemies of one race as the other, to cozen, beguile, and use
> the negroes . . . . . In the villages the negroes were the office
> holders, men who knew none of the uses of authority except
> its insolences.
>
> Woodrow Wilson

---

[11]For a full discussion of historical misrepresentations, see John Hope Franklin's "*Birth of a Nation*: Propaganda as History." In this essay, Franklin details the distortion of events in South Carolina during Reconstruction.

¶. . . .The policy of the congressional leaders wrought . . . a veritable overthrow of civilization in the South . . . . . in their determination to <u>put the white South under the heel of the black South</u>.

Woodrow Wilson

¶ The white men were roused by a mere instinct of self-preservation . . . . . until at last there had sprung into existence a great Ku Klux Klan, a veritable empire of the South, to protect the Southern country.

Woodrow Wilson

These title cards are followed immediately by another, which does not carry Woodrow Wilson's name, but which by virtue of association carries the same authority:

¶ The Uncrowned King. [Austin Stoneman]

¶ The executive mansion of the nation had shifted from the White House to this strange house on Capitol Hill.

The implication of this sequencing is that all statements are factual and that all carry the same weight as the history written by the U.S. president. The suspect nature of Wilson's history in terms of adherence to fact would not have been within the purview of many movie goers, large numbers of whom embraced the same attitudes about race as Wilson and many of whom did not, in any case, enjoy lives that encouraged them to read.

Considering the weight given to his words, it is small wonder that Wilson said the movie was "like writing history with lightning," concluding ". . . my only regret is that it is all so terribly true" (Franklin 47). If some of the lightning Wilson perceived came from the pleasure of seeing his own words on the screen, a great deal must also have come from the spectacle and movement, the remarkable excitement of backlit figures moving across the screen like the projections of Wilson's own imagined *History*, a work with which the film shares its comfortingly racist attitudes.

The problem with this movie, however, does not rest in attitude alone. Misrepresentations of events are deliberately manipulated in *The Birth of a Nation* to produce an illusion of truth that often contradicts historical evidence. One example is in the use of "historical facsimiles" within the movie. Three such historical facsimiles are Ford's theater, where the audience witnesses Lincoln's assassination; Appomattox Courthouse, where the audience witnesses Lee's surrender; and the State House of Representatives of South Carolina. Each of these is introduced by a title card identifying the setting as a facsimile based on a historical documentation.

In the first two facsimiles, the events presented match the publically known and verifiable facts. Unfortunately, this kind of historical presentation is not consistently employed by the film's creators. Thus, in the third historical facsimile, the movie asserts[12] that the House of Representatives was occupied by a helpless minority of 23 whites while the hundred plus black members took off their shoes, ate chicken, swilled liquor, and passed a law permitting the intermarriage of blacks and whites while the black lawmakers stared lewdly at the white women spectators in the gallery. When the movie claims that the legislative setting is another "historical facsimile" it implies that the events are also historically accurate. Yet there is no historical foundation for this scenario. It is easy to understand why for Gerald Mast and Bruce Kawn these scenes are among the "most objectionable" in the entire movie (67).

Apparently, Dixon's purpose in bringing the filmed version of his novel to the

---

[12]"An HISTORICAL FACSIMILE of the State House of Representatives as it was in 1870. After a photograph by the Columbia State" (*The Birth of a Nation*").

public was not historical truth at all.[13] According to an interview cited by Elliott

Carter:

> "one purpose . . .was to create a feeling of abhorrence in people,
> especially white women, against colored men"; [and another] "that he
> wished to have Negroes removed from the United States and that he
> hopes to help in the accomplishment of that purpose by *The Birth of*
> *a Nation*."   ("Fighting a Vicious Film" . . . 79)

There can be no question that Dixon's desires were at least partially fulfilled.
The Birth of a Nation attracted huge audiences, and ended up earning an
unprecedented figure of between $10,000,000.00 and $14,000,000.00 on its initial
investment of $110,000.00 (Gianetti and Eyman 15).   The movie had earned
$18,000,000.00 by the time the first talkies were released (Dilks 1).

On February 15, 1915, the movie was first screened in New York as *The*
Clansman. So powerful was the audience response to the emotionally packed epic at
this premiere that Dixon insisted the name be changed to *The Birth of a Nation*.
Subsequent to its opening under the new title on March 3, 1915, the movie was
shown 6,266 times in New York alone to a conservatively estimated 3,000,000
viewers (Guerrero 13; Carter 9). It would subsequently be shown in thousands of
theaters throughout the nation.

Given its inflammatory nature, no one should be surprised that the movie
attracted extremely vocal and active groups of partisans and opponents. Dixon, no
stranger to opposition, enlisted the aid of his old school friend Woodrow Wilson, now
president of the United States, arranging to screen *The Birth of a Nation* for him at
the White House.

Dixon also sought to screen the movie for the Supreme Court. After an initial

---

[13]The dedication of Dixon's novel, *The Clansman*, reads "To the memory of a Scotch-
Irish leader of the South, my Uncle, Colonel Leroy McAfee, Grand Titan of the
Invisible Empire of the Ku Klux Klan" (qtd. Carter 10).

rebuff, he was encouraged in this effort by the Chief Justice, himself a former member of the Klan. Thus, according to John Hope Franklin, "not only were members of the Supreme Court ". . . to see the picture, but many members of the Senate and House of Representatives were also there with their guests" (47). This meant that *The Birth of a Nation* had, at the very least, the *de facto* endorsement of the highest legislative officials in America. Dixon hoped that such an endorsement would enable the film to prosper despite the significant boycotts and protests mounted by the NAACP and he was not disappointed.

Overcoming the best efforts of its opponents, Griffith's film was rarely suppressed, although the director did remove approximately nine minutes of film (Mast and Kawn 66) consisting of 558 feet of film "showing black soldiers attacking white women" (Guerrero 14). In fact, it is recorded that the Ku Klux Klan, more or less moribund prior to the movie's advent, was revived in Georgia on the basis of the movie's inflammatory impact. No fewer than 25,000 Klansmen in full regalia marched down Peachtree Street in Atlanta to celebrate the opening there of Griffith's movie (Guerrero 14). In one Southern theater, the crowd was so enthusiastic that they actually "shot up the screen" (Franklin 50) in a frenzy of participatory enthusiasm as the "Aryan race" (*The Birth of a Nation)* rose in its own defense.

What is left when the dust has settled is a movie that still retains great power due to its technical proficiency and innovations, as well as to its still inflammatory racial bias. It is at best the "record of a cultural illusion"(Carter 15)[14] and not, despite its claims, of history itself. There are numerous illustrative examples, ranging from the historically inaccurate spectacle of a marauding Negro regiment despoiling the Cameron home to the ludicrous vision of the South Carolina House of

---

[14]Part of the cultural illusion at work can be seen in the racist casting practices employed by Griffith. Black roles of greater importance to the plot development, such as those of Lydia Brown, Silas Lynch, and Gus, were played by white actors in blackface. That the blackface tradition was inherited from the vaudeville stage in no way alters its racist implications, particularly in a movie where black actors and extras were employed in crowd scenes.

Representatives.

Even before the movie's start, the audience sees one of Griffith's title cards.

A PLEA FOR THE ART OF THE MOTION PICTURE

We do not fear censorship, for we have no wish to offend with improprieties or obscenities, but we do demand, as a right the liberty to show the dark side of wrong, that we may illuminate the bright side of virtue - the same liberty that is conceded to the art of the written word - that art to which we owe the Bible and the works of Shakespeare.   *(The Birth of a Nation)*

Particularly chilling about *The Birth of a Nation* are its claim to *be* history and the effect that claim has had upon thousands, very probably millions, of viewers whose subsequent understanding of American history was shaped less by any reality than by the movie's deliberate misconstruction of events and their meanings. Even today, the battlefield scenes carry the same power as the famous Brady photographs, bringing the viewer into the experience of war in immediate and powerful ways. Yet the same movie promulgates historical lies as facts. Griffith himself apparently never understood why the charges of racism were leveled against the movie (Giannetti and Eyman 16). Dixon reveled in the movie's effect on the American populace.

Prior to *The Birth of a Nation*, the world had not yet fully envisioned the power of feature length movies to sway the emotions or even their power to attract audiences. Questions of accuracy and free expression raised by the film continue be debated today. If the movie's influence on the mainstream plantation genre film now seems predictable, other effects seem less so.

The rise of independent black film companies could hardly have been a goal of Dixon or of Griffith, yet these companies were indeed formed and clearly arose in response to *The Birth of a Nation*. 1916 saw the creation of the Lincoln Motion Picture Company. 1918 saw both the release of *The Birth of a Race* (the first independent film production of Booker T. Washington's personal secretary, Emmett

J. Scott) and the beginning of Oscar Micheaux's now legendary career as an independent black filmmaker. Less predictable, also, though it would appeal more to Dixon, is the fact that the film is in use today as "a recruitment piece for Klan membership" (Dilks 1).

The trenchant lesson here is that the movies do not merely reflect their times and societies. They influence them in profound and unpredictable ways. *The Birth of a Nation* is, at best, a paradoxical exercise of freedom of expression, one we do well to examine for context as well as for content.

Works Cited

Carter, Elliot. "Cultural History Written with Lightning: The Significance of *The Birth of a Nation.*" Peter C. Rollins, ed. *Hollywood as Historian.* Kentucky: University of Kentucky Press, 1983. 9-19.

Dilks, Tim. "The Birth of a Nation (1915)." 5 August 2000 <http://www.filmsite.org/birt.html>.

"Fighting a Vicious Film: Protest against "The Birth of a Nation." Boston Branch of the National Association for the Advancement of Colored People, 1915. Mintz and Roberts, 79-80.

Franklin, John Hope. *"Birth of a Nation–Propaganda as History."* Mintz and Roberts, 42-53.

Giannetti, Louis and Scott Eyman. *Flashback: A Brief History of Film.* Englewood Cliffs, NJ: Prentice Hall, 1996.

Guerrero, Ed. *Framing Blackness.* Philadelphia: Temple University Press, 1993.

Mast, Gerald and Bruce F. Kawn. *A Short History of the Movies.* Boston: Allyn and Bacon, 2000.

Mintz, Steven and Randy Roberts, eds. *Hollywood's America.* New York: Brandywine Press, 1993.

The Birth of a Nation. Dir. David W. Griffith. With Lillian Gish, Mae Marsh, David B. Walthall. David W. Griffith Corp., Epoch Producing Company. 1915.

When Rubber Meets the Road:
Thelma and Louise and *Leaving Normal* as
Complementary Cultural Texts

Brains'll only get you so far and luck always runs out.
—Hal Slocum
Thelma and Louise

Thelma and Louise, written by Callie Khouri and directed by Ridley Scott, was released in 1991. Telling the story of two women, a waitress (Susan Sarandon) and an abused younger wife (Geena Davis) on a weekend trip to "get away," the movie treats its audience to a nightmare of gender based persecution as the innocent weekend turns into a near epidemic of crime. The movie's theatrical release generated an astonishing amount of heated and, I thought at the time, remarkable responses from reviewers and op-ed writers alike. A year later, the release of the thematically related *Leaving Normal,* written by Ed Soloman and directed by Edward Zwick, which also featured a waitress and an abused young wife on the road in a convertible, was largely dismissed as fluff, generating none of the heat prompted by Thelma and Louise. *Leaving Normal,* for example, was dismissed by *Entertainment Weekly* as "a female buddy movie with a soft runny center" (1) and described by Brian Johnson as ". . . too cute and contrived—which is a shame, because the performances are charged with improvisational energy" (Johnson, *Leaving Normal* 1).

Far more eye catching are a number of the early responses to *Thelma and Louise* quoted by Richard Schickel in his cover story for *Time* on June 24, 1991. The vehemence and variety of these responses are a clear demonstration that the movie had struck a very sensitive cultural nerve. Depending on who is being quoted, the movie is either a wonderful film illuminated by feminist consciousness or else a cheap attempt to glorify violent crime as long as it is committed by women.

". . . the first movie . . .which told the downright truth" says Mary Lucey, a lesbian activist in Los Angeles.

". . . a paean to transformative violence . . . An explicit fascist theme," writes . . . John Leo . . . in *U.S. News and World Report*.

"It is, according to Cathy Bell . . . once married to a 'a redneck control freak . . . like seeing my life played before my eyes.'"

"It justifies armed robbery, manslaughter and chronic drunken driving as exercises in consciousness raising," charges *New York Daily News* Columnist Richard Johnson.

It is, according to *Miami Herald* movie reviewer Bill Cosford, "a butt kicking feminist manifesto . . .which sweeps you along for the ride."

(Schickel, Cover Story 1)

Clearly, there was a lot of intense reaction to this story of two women on the road together, this pair of "vigilantes with vaginas" (Emerson 1). And though one is tempted to be satisfied with the easy observation that the positive responses came mostly from women and the negative mostly from men, the reactions expressed deserve more consideration than that.

In Scott's *Thelma and Louise*, a fortyish waitress named Louise Sawyer (Susan Sarandon) and her friend Thelma (Geena Davis), the young and naive wife of an abusive husband, are taking a weekend trip to another friend's cabin. Though neither of them knows anything about fishing—the weekend's ostensible goal—both desperately need a little time off from their respective relationships.

Thelma's marriage is a perfect comic example of a relationship driven by a repressive, self-absorbed, and ignorant husband. Louise's relationship with her boyfriend, a lounge musician unwilling to commit, is illustrative of a dilemma frequently faced by the no-longer-young woman in a society that treats her as a commodity.

In the course of their trip to the cabin, Thelma is nearly raped by a roadhouse Casanova. The rape is prevented by Louise, who (in the sort of coincidence we seem to enjoy shamelessly in fiction and film) is carrying in her bag the gun Thelma brought along for safety but was too nervous to carry herself, the gun bought for her by her husband. Importantly, Louise doesn't pull the trigger and kill the would-be rapist until the danger is past, finally pushed beyond the limit of her control by his arrogance and taunts.

The rest of the movie has the two women on the run from the law, interacting along the way with a petty thief named JD (Brad Pitt) who seduces Thelma and steals all their money, a repellent truckdriver (whose truck they destroy), and a bullying state cop (whom they lock in the trunk of his cruiser). They have become felons wanted for murder and armed robbery who will ultimately escape capture by driving off a cliff into the Grand Canyon. The movie closes with a freeze frame of Louise's Thunderbird convertible in flight.

Even in 1991, a year now fast receding into the last century, I wondered what all the flap was really about. Certainly context was important, along with critical point of view—whether feminist, masculinist, or film-historical. Not surprisingly, most of the visible critics of the film worked from one or more of these bases, which accounts in part for the preponderance of comparisons of *Thelma and Louise* with Butch Cassidy and the *Sundance Kid*.

Thus, for instance, we can point to Ralph Novak's anti-feminist statement that

70

a "movie that went as far out of its way to trash women as this female chauvinist sow of a film does to trash men would be universally, and justifiably, condemned" (1). We can also point to John Simon's assertion, rooted in two contexts of antifeminism and film history:

> . . . this overlong, underrealized, and overmanicured movie reflects the deludedness of its makers. They think that, by exultantly sacrificing their lives, Thelma and Louise somehow justify their anti-social anabasis. They think that feminist liberation, even if hurtling into destructive excess, is somehow glorious, which is surely the way benighted moviegoers are encouraged to view it. But it leaves a bad taste in the thinking mind, as did *Butch Cassidy, Easy Rider, Sugarland Express,* and countless others." (Simon 5)

In the same vein, there is *Time 's* rather curious offering:

> As a bulletin from the front in the battle of the sexes, *Thelma and Louise* sends the message that little ground has been won. For these two women, feminism never happened. Thelma and Louise are so trapped that the only way for them to get away [is to be free]– wildly, self-destructively so – free to drive off the ends of the earth . . . . free to behave like –, men[1]. . . . At least *Thelma and Louise* stop short of

---

[1]This presupposes that violence and self-destruction are male characteristics, and as such not credible as female modes of behavior. The evidence, at least the textual evidence discussed in this essay, suggests that such a view is devoted to questionable beliefs about gender and behavior. Motive, however, is something else. Butch and Sundance choose their mode of life largely out of a sense of boredom with civilization–for that is the impression they give—whereas Thelma and Louise base their choices on the accumulation of circumstances that makes their behavior a logical choice. The words and action of Etta Place, who accompanies Butch and Sundance because her position as an unmarried schoolteacher with no prospects is unendurable, supports the interpretation of Butch and Sundance as rejecting civilization because, like Huck Finn, they have seen what it has to offer and found it wanting. Even for Etta, outlawry was preferable to her other choices in society. There is a serious perceived dissonance—or was in 1991—between womanhood and the jolly pair of outlaws, a dissonance that prompted Jim Emerson (in a flurry of hyphenations) to

emulating Butch Cassidy and the Sundance Kid, who use their remaining ammunition to go out in a blaze of testosteronic glory. (Carlson 1)

More socially cognizant and more perceptive are the words of Brian Johnson and Richard Schickel, both of whom recognize the narrative and cinematic relationship between *Thelma and Louise* and *Butch Cassidy and the Sundance Kid*.

And in its own modest way, *Thelma & Louise* breaks new ground for American cinema. While recalling the renegade romance of Bonnie and Clyde (1967), the despair of *Easy Rider* (1969), and the sunbaked banter of *Butch Cassidy and the Sundance Kid* (1969) it puts a sassy, feminist spin on the outlaw myth." (Johnson 64)

With Butch and Sundance, as it works out, we are looking at a set of characters—actually one character doubled by another—that emerges as early in American Literature as James Fenimore Cooper's *Leatherstocking Tales*. In Cooper, the pair is presented in terms of light and dark—European and Indian in colonial America. In later literary manifestations the pair takes on a more antic quality (the white Huck Finn and Tom Sawyer, Huck Finn and escaped black slave Jim) as one of the partners pursues his own whimsical and often humorous way while his sidekick comes along as ballast. This picaresque pair has traditionally been represented as male. The emergence of female "buddies" is a strikingly recent event American popular culture. So while there is much echo of "Butch & Sundance" in *Thelma and Louise*—the humorous dialog, the outlawry with its attendant scenes of pursuit—there is a gender consciousness at work in Scott's film that seriously undercuts the stereotype of the romanticized outlaws as folk heroes.

It is nearly a cliché, in 2001, to point out that outlaws had a tremendous appeal to 1960's film audiences, but it is an important point to remember. It is equally

---

write "Gender-switching a traditional male-oriented genre is an intriguing place to start, but *Thelma and Louise* only key-scratches at the lustrous surface, and then takes a joy ride off into the pre-fab, picture-pretty sunset" (3).

important to remember that the outlaws were, in terms of who dominated the outlaw journey, male.

> The '60's gave us Bonnie and Clyde, Butch and Sundance . . . *Thelma and Louise* is a sign that things are looking up in the '90's. . . . *Thelma and Louise* is the first important movie to plop two women in a car and send them careening down open Western roads with the cops in wheel-spinning pursuit. And it is the first movie to use sexism as the motivating force for their misdeeds. (Schickel, Review 64)

Indeed, Richard Schickel provides one of the more balanced and thoughtful responses from 1991.

> . . . anyone with a sense of recent film history can see *Thelma and Louise* in the honorable line of movies whose makers, without quite knowing what they were doing, sank a drill into what appeared to be familiar American soil and found that they had somehow tapped into a wild-rushing subterranean stream of inchoate outrage and deranged violence. (Cover Story 2)

It is this "subterranean stream," I believe, that gives *Thelma and Louise* its power and its credibility while denying the same strengths to *Leaving Normal*. But the stream is somewhat more complex in nature than Schickel suggests. While he is right that "these films tend to serve as expressions of the values or confusions jangling around in their society, or occasionally as springboards for earnest discussion of them" (Cover Story 2), he does not take into account the sources that might fuel such discussion. By 1995, this earnest discussion to which he refers had expanded to include the academy as scholars recognized narrative patterns in the film that seemed to replicate earlier American texts. To the contexts already mentioned was added the history of American Literature.

In a paper titled "Thelma and Louise in the Wilderness:—or—Butch Cassidy and Jonathan Edwards in Drag," presented at the Northeast Popular Culture Association in October 1995, David R. Williams argued that ". . . the elite texts of one generation influence the popular culture of the next" (1). He continued with the assertion that "Elite culture is always *avant garde*, always in rebellion against tradition, always rejecting the past. It has to be if it is to stay ahead of the mob" (1).

In support of this premise, he offered a somewhat controversial reading of *Thelma and Louise*, locating the movie not so much in the context of 90's feminist theory and criticism or even film history as in the double contexts of patriarchal American Puritan narrative, which relates the journey of the faithful into the wilderness of sin, and that strain of conventional (and masculinist) American Literature generally identified as literature of the frontier, a strain in which the hero's self-realization is the result of a simultaneous journey into the wilderness of American continent and the wilderness of his own consciousness.

In Williams' reading, which insists on what may be loosely termed "larger contexts" for the film, we find a model that establishes the central narrative of the American Puritan culture as the journey of the individual sinner, representative of the chosen people, into the wilderness. There, the worldly structures that contain these travelers, what Williams calls their "old dependencies," are abandoned, and they achieve a mystical insight. Of *Thelma and Louise*, Williams writes that the movie is "in short, a conversion narrative, a modern 'Narrative of the Captivity of Mary Rowlandson' all the more powerful because the imagery and language and setting and plot fit the traditional pattern perfectly without overt mention ever being made" (3).[2]

This same wilderness journey that animated the puritan narrative, Williams maintains, is embedded in American Literature so deeply and pervasively that it has

---

[2]Technically, Williams is conflating two rather different narratives here. The conversion narrative and the captivity narrative, though they share in the same rhetoric, tell exceedingly different stories. The first is the story of the Christian soul's coming to grace; the second is the story of the abduction and subsequent ransom of a Puritan settler by hostile Indians. Though the two types of "redemption" overlap in Puritan thought, they can hardly be said to be identical.

produced a range of notable figures, some more legendary than literary, that ranges from Huck Finn[3] and Jim to Butch Cassidy and the Sundance Kid.

Thus far, the argument is both provocative and intriguing. To assert, however, as Williams does, that Thelma and Louise are "Butch Cassidy and Jonathan Edwards in drag" is an oversimplification that ignores the deep meaning of gender in the film and in the earlier narratives, like Mary White Rowlandson's. Given that Williams cites these narrative sources (part of the "submerged stream" posited by Richard Schickel) for the film's power, he treats them on a disappointingly surface level. It is not a dismissable coincidence that most of the surviving conversion narratives from the puritan era were authored by men.

The power of the pen was largely confined to puritan men and though women were expected to read they were not expected to exercise authorial literacy in public documents.[4] The conversion narrative (the narrative of coming to Christ) served primarily as proof and documentation that a candidate for membership in the Church of Visible Saints had been truly converted. As such, it is distinct from the captivity narratives which emerged later in the course of American puritan literature, and which encapsulate the rhetoric of conversion in the relatively secular story of captivity by hostile Indians.

Thus, it is a crucial point that the early captivity narratives which are most

---

[3]Arguably, Huck Finn owes his nature as much to the European picaresque hero as he does to the wilderness journeys of the American puritans.

[4]Thus, for example, the majority of female conversion narratives, which were presented not to the full congregation (though male narratives were) but to the minister in private, in keeping with views of feminine modesty, were not recorded at all. Thomas Sheperd, however, transcribed a number of them in a sort of personal shorthand, believing it was part of his obligation as a pastor. Small wonder then, that when Anne Bradstreet's poems were first published, they had to be smuggled out of her puritan settlement to London, where they were initially published through the agency of her brother-in-law.

widely referred to[5], like those of Mary White Rowlandson, Hannah Swarton, and Hannah Dustan, are the stories of women who, outside the confines of their puritan communities, captives to people whose language and customs they did not share, were forced and in an odd way enabled to figure themselves against the wilderness landscape in ways that had never before been possible to them. Partly because they were no longer protected by (dependent on) their men, they were enabled, however subtly, to question and even to condemn the "old dependencies" by which they were finally to be redeemed from captivity.

Given this additional information about some of the earliest American literary narratives, which were, incidentally, very much a part of the popular culture, we can expand our understanding of *Thelma and Louise*. Like the female authors of the puritan captivity narratives, Thelma and Louise are women creating their own narrative[6]—their own lives—as the movie unfolds.

In this process, they echo and amplify the gender-based criticisms implicit in Mary White Rowlandson's work. In her original "Narrative of the Captivity . . ." Rowlandson excoriates the British soldiers who fail to deliver her and her fellow

---

[5]To be sure, the captivity narrative was not the exclusive property of women who wrote. Such women, as already noted, were relatively uncommon. This explains why the line "written in her own hand" appeared on the cover of Rowlandson's book. A telling example of the male captivity narrative is "The Redeemed Captive Returning to Zion" by John Williams. In this narrative, the male narrator, who is a minister, retains a posture of authority even when threatened with the loss of his children and his own life, a posture not adopted by the women who had similar experiences but no access to the pulpit as a means of sharing and explicating the meaning of their captivities.

[6]One crucial difference, of course, is that Thelma and Louise exist only as scripted characters, not as real people in real situations. This, however, is part of the nature of art, in popular culture and elite culture alike. What was real becomes a more or less deeply submerged part of cultural knowledge, re-enacted in subsequent art with varying degrees of adherence to the original event(s). In a way, Thelma and Louise are rather like saints embracing their own destruction to encourage others to change their lives, a role that fell to those women of the Church of Visible Saints who generated the Indian captivity narratives referred to by Williams..

captives. Subsequent to her redemption from captivity, during which she suffered the death of one of her daughters, she was unable to embrace completely the values of the community from which she had been abducted. Even when the state declared an official day of thanksgiving for her, she felt that she had cause to mourn. Her words, "I can remember the time, when I used to sleep quietyly without workings in my thoughts, whole nights together. . ." (229) are as compelling today as when they were first published in 1682. Like the fictional Thelma, she might have said that "something crossed over in me" (*Thelma and Louise*). Like Thelma in her own wilderness, Mary Rowlandson had been irrevocably changed by removal from her society. While neither Thelma nor Louise is abducted by hostile Indians (or gangsters, or any other likely Hollywood suspect), the two of them together enact the recurrent sense in Rowlandson's text that patriarchal organization has failed them, that it does not understand them and cannot rescue them from the physical and psychological chain of events that has been set in motion.

The characters of Thelma and Louise also present a variant on the narrative of Hannah Dustan. A congregant of Cotton Mather, Dustan was delivered from Indian captivity not by ransom or rescue from the puritan settlement, but by her own hand. Seeing, apparently, no hope but within herself for rescue or escape, Dustan inspired her fellow captives to join her in uprising. She returned home with Indian scalps dangling from her belt, was remunerated by a grateful government, and was given notably short shrift in Mather's account of her adventures in the wilderness.[7]

In terms of narrative strategy then, Dustan's story—rendered in the third person by a narrator who was not present for its events—is closer to that of *Thelma*

---

[7]In a volume entitled *Humiliations Followed by Deliverances*, published in 1697, puritan minister Cotton Mather related, in first person, the Indian captivity narratives of several puritan women, all of whom but Hannah Dustan had been redeemed by conventional methods—ransom or other negotiation. All of these narratives except that of Hannah Dustan, whose actions placed her outside the day's conception of womanhood, were rendered in the first person. Dustan's relatively short narrative was rendered in the third person, a rhetorically distancing strategy that today seems painfully obvious.

and Louise than is Rowlandson's. Dustan's story, like that of Thelma and Louise, is to some extent scripted by an outside agency. Also like that of Thelma and Louise, Dustan's narrative is the story of woman moving so far outside her contemporary definitions of femininity that she becomes terrifying to at least some elements of her own society. Dustan's action in killing her abductors, some described as children, lay far beyond the boundaries of acceptable behavior for a woman. Even the murder of her own newborn by her abductors does not fully excuse her. Yet her popular fame was such that her narrative could not successfully be suppressed. So if we enlarge Williams' argument to include specific texts, we can see a rather forceful continuous line of American female narrative in which gender is crucial to the narrative's meaning and to its posture.

Unlike Hannah Dustan, Thelma and Louise are not able to return home and be rewarded for the real and metaphorical scalps hanging from their belts. This fact alone suggests a hardening of the same "old dependencies" that have had Americans (real and fictional) from Natty Bumppo to Calamity Jane, from Huck Finn to Jeremiah Johnson, abandoning civilization. It is not solely the Daniel Boone-esque and masculine concept of "elbow room" that motivates women constructing their lives and life stories. It is the need (sometimes forced upon them by circumstance) to step *outside* the structures of civilization—worldly or otherwise—in order to achieve themselves.

A complementary, or perhaps corollary, cinematic cultural text to *Thelma and Louise* is Edward Zwick's 1992 release, *Leaving Normal*. Like Thelma and Louise, the women in question are a young wife, Marianne (played by Meg Tilly) on the run from an abusive husband and an older, far more savvy woman, Darly (played by Christine Lahti). Darly is a waitress by trade and her past, like that of Louise, contains a terrible, almost unspeakable secret. Like the journey of Thelma and Louise, their journey of Marianne and Darly is punctuated by meetings with various interesting and appalling characters, and by a profusion of panoramic shots which serve to frame smaller units within the narrative. The similarities are sufficient, in fact, to have caused Roger Ebert to write:

> I've made a heroic effort to consider *Leaving Normal* on its own, but
> I cannot rid my mind of *Thelma and Louise*. It is not the fault of
> *Leaving Normal* that it resembles a better film released less than a
> year earlier, but there you have it. As two women hit the road in an
> attempt to escape their pasts, the echo of the earlier, better film
> sounds in almost every scene. (1)

Once again, we must enter that "subterranean stream" of Schickel's. What Ebert
misses, in his reading of one film in the context of another, is that *Leaving Normal* is
actually part of a different genre that partakes of a shared cultural history in very
different ways. Unlike the dramatic narrative of *Thelma and Louise,* the unifying
generic foundation of *Leaving Normal* is the fairy tale, that "Once upon a time . . ."
invitation to a dimension where people can end by living "happily ever after,"[8] an
option not accessible to Thelma and Louise.

Thus, while the domestic violence suffered by Marianne is every bit as awful
as that suffered by Thelma and in actually more physically brutal, Marianne continues
to believe in the possibility of heterosexual romance and continues to search for it.
In this, she bears a superficial resemblance to Thelma, with her strong attraction to
JD. In the circumstances faced by Thelma and Louise, however, matters were so clear
that even the besotted Thelma could not misread the reality—JD was an opportunist
and thief and a sexist to boot who, given the opportunity, loved and left his women,
having stolen from them all he could—love, money, and whatever else he can.

---

[8]As if the happy endings of Darly and Marianne were not enough, both incidentally
earned by female figures *conforming* to received notions of womanhood, Zwick gives
us, in mid-film, the encapsulated story of Cece (played by Patrika Darbo), a waitress
whose work is serving food, nurturing, if you will, all comers. She is fat, plain, and
something of an airhead–but she believes in the possibilities of romance and, sure
enough, is discovered and swept off her feet by a Canadian "prince charming." They
dance far into the night under a canopy of stars and then embark on their "happily
ever after" exit–a remarkably strong echo of the Cinderella tale, and one impossible
to read as anything *but* a fairy tale.

Like her fellow waitress Louise, Darly carries a terrible secret but unlike Louise she has not suffered a rape. She has been victimized by a husband who deserted her and has, in turn, deserted her own child in an effort to survive in a hostile world. Yet like Louise, and like Mary Rowlandson with her fellow captive (Goodwife Josline), Darly is a protective presence in the life of the other woman who accompanies her. Darly will even, by the movie's end, initiate a search for her missing daughter,[9] thus placing herself back within the accepted boundaries of behavior for a woman. She has acknowledged her own maternal failure and becomes, instead of the woman who abandons her child, the good mother who seeks her child against tremendous odds.

Unlike Thelma and Louise, Darly and Marianne are able, with hard work and a fair measure of emotional wrangling, to establish that most American of desires, a home in the wilderness. This home first appears, appropriately enough, as a house without walls or roof, an open foundation that Darly furnishes for the audience with her recollections of earlier dreams. If these dreams are limited, partaking in equal parts of the sentimental and the middle class, they are nonetheless part of the fairy tale equation which insists that women embrace socially determined norms if they are to survive. At the same time, this house in the Alaskan wilderness is the antithesis of houses visited earlier in the film—the bungalow of Marianne's second abusive husband, the upscale yuppie nightmare of Marianne's sister and her husband, even the claustrophobic trailer of Cece (nicknamed "66"). If Cece is the embodiment of the fairy tale at the heart of the movie, the princess who finds her prince, she is also something of a fairy godmother, giving the trailer to Darly and Marianne so that they can finish their own journeys.

---

[9] In this, too, she is like Rowlandson, some of whose children remained in captivity in the wilderness, lost to her and a source of grief only a little less than that she felt for her dead child. This theme, incidentally, recurs innumerable times in women's captivity narratives. Because the rediscovery and recovery of her child is possible, Darly is more fortunate, more capable of the "happily ever after" ending than either Thelma and Louise or her literary predecessors in narratives of Indian captivity.

To be sure, *Leaving Normal* and *Thelma and Louise* both encapsulate the motif of the journey into the wilderness. That men are killed in reprisal in *Thelma and Louise* but not in *Leaving Normal* marks, to some extent, the generic differences of the two movies. If we discount the Darly's long-gone and never-on-screen husband, the most intransigent of the men portrayed in Darly's life is Walt, an Alaskan who offers her a munificent $500.00 to dance and strip for him. Ultimately, however, he is helpless to contend with Darly's despair, a despair that is the inevitable consequence of the frontier culture Walt represents. The result, in this instance, is that Walt relents, giving her the money without collecting what he has paid for.

In the home that Darly and Marianne finally create, the adults are women and the children are men, two native American adolescents who are on their own as a result of the cultural depredations of Euro-American civilization. Both Darly and Marianne, at their cores, are women who love men, and who seek a way to exist that can encompass both male and female without destroying either one. In this they are distinct from Thelma and Louise, who may hunger for men but who ultimately reject lengthy relationships with them, knowing that society has made these relationships impossible to sustain.

The geography of the American southwest, the huge, inhumanly beautiful sweep of landscape that frames the journey of Thelma and Louise, is replaced in *Leaving Normal* by the panorama of the heavens, the broad canopy of stars that marks a youngster's sense of wonder. This device is so heavily affected that Brian Johnson, apparently moved by the movie's fairy tale effect even if he did not fullyy articulate it, felt compelled to note the ". . . gaudy display of northern lights [that] completes the When You Wish Upon a Star sense of wonder" (Johnson, *Leaving Normal* 2)

This difference brings us back to Roger Ebert and other reviewers who seem to read movies exclusively from an appropriate but intellectually limiting film historical point of view. Ebert is, characteristically, unconcerned with the cultural antecedents of film beyond the contexts suggested by other films. David Williams seeks to locate film as a cultural text in the broader literary traditions of America—an effort deserving hearty applause, though the use of such a broad canvas can encourage a certain blurring of detail.

This is, in the case of gender conscious movies, a dangerous pitfall. Neither *Thelma and Louise* nor Marianne and Darly can reasonably be categorized as male heroes in drag. They are, for one thing, women. For another, they are conscious of their gender and all the worldly considerations that implies.

To conclude, like Roger Ebert, that no men are killed in *Leaving Normal* simply because the script writer is male is to ignore the genre of the film. Fairy tales, even the most contemporary, do not make the survival and happiness of their central figures impossible to achieve.

At the same time, to maintain with David Williams that today's popular culture derives from yesterday's elite culture is somewhat misleading. If the Indian captivity narratives of the sixteen and seventeen hundreds had by the twentieth century become part of elite culture, a property of the student of literary history, they nonetheless came into being squarely in the territory of *popular* culture, and have not, I believe, ever entirely left that location. Instead, they have been echoed, replicated, and modified by succeeding generations of narrative as succeeding generations of humanity have grappled with (among other things) the gender issues these narratives embody.

Taken together, *Thelma and Louise* and *Leaving Normal* provide cultural texts that explode the cultural myth of the happy little woman. Both demonstrate a vividly contemporary realization that women are tremendously strong and resilient, whether as the figures of Thelma and Louise flying a Thunderbird simultaneously into the Grand Canyon and mythic status, or as Darly and Marianne assuming the role of adults in the wilderness home whose promise has always lured people into the vastness of America.

Surely it is no accident that one story offers women the option to submit or die, and the other removes them from "old dependencies" to a frontier where men may succumb to noble sentiment and where Indians, instead of taking captives, come into the house where the women are adults, responsible for their own own destinies and their own dreams.

Works Cited

Carlson, Margaret. *"Thelma and Louise." Time.* June 24, 1991 v136 n25 p57(1). 5
October 2000 <http://library.usca.sc.edu/research/discus.html>.

Ebert. Roger. *"Leaving Normal* (review)." Chicago Sun-Times. April 29, 1992.

Emerson, Jim. *"Thelma and Louise* (review). 8 October 2000
<http://cinepad.com/reviews/thelma.htm>.

Gleiberman, Own. *"Leaving Normal* (review)." *Entertainment Weekly,* May 22, 1992
n119 p55(1). 5 October 2000
<http://library.usca.sc.edu/research/discus.html>.

Johnson, Brian D. *"Leaving Normal* (review)." *Maclean's,* May 11, 1992, v105 n 19
p58(1). 5 October 2000 <http://library.usca.sc.edu/research/discus.html>.

Johnson, Brian D. *"Thelma and Louise* (review)." *Maclean's.* May 27, 1991, v104
n21 p64(1). 5 October 2000 <http://library.usca.sc.edu/research/discus.html>.

Leaving Normal. Dir. Edward Zwick. Wr. Edward Solomon. With Christine Lahti,
Meg Tilly. Mirage Engertainment. 1992.

Novak, Ralph. *"Thelma and Louise* (review)." *People Weekly.* June 10, 1991 v35 n22
p10(1). 5 October 2000 <http://library.usca.sc.edu/research/discus.html>.

Rowlandson, Mary White. "A Narrative of the Captivity and Restauration of Mrs.
Mary Rowlandson. Giles Gunn, ed. *Early American Writing.*NY: Penguin
Books, 1994. 217-31.

Schickel, Richard. *"Thelma and Louise* (cover story)." *Time,* June 24, 1991 v137 n25
p52(5).

Schickel, Richard. *"Thelma and* Louise (review)." *Time.* May 27, 1991. v137 n21
64(1).

Simon, John. *"Thelma and Louise* (review)." *National Review,* July 8, 1991. v43 n12
P48(3). 5 October 2000 <http://library.usca.sc.edu/research/discus.html>.

Thelma and Louise. Dir. Ridley Scott. Wr. Callie Khouri. With Susan Sarandon,
Geena Davis. MGM/UA. 1991.

84

Williams, David R. "Thelma and Louise in the Wilderness: -or- Butch Cassidy and Jonathan Edwards in Drag." A paper presented at the Northeast Popular Culture Association Conference. Worcester, Massachusetts. October, 1995.

Will the Real Fairy Godmother Please Stand Up?

This is not a masquerade. This is real life.

—*Noxeema Jackson*
To Wong Foo, Thanks for Everything! Julie Newmar

An old expression assures us that there is more than one way to skin a cat. No doubt that is true. And, of course, there is more than one way to tell a story. The same story, seen through different eyes, voiced through a different set of lips, refined by a different sense of taste, rendered in a different medium, tinted more softly or more violently pronounced, can vary considerably from its initial version. Yet there remains a body of shared material in those different versions that makes comparison inevitable for anyone who encounters a story in more than one guise. In no two media that I can think of is a given story more likely to be re-told than in literature and film.

It has become something of a commonplace to talk about not bothering with a book because one has seen the movie, or vice versa. This rather unnerving position is frequently adopted by my students in both film and literature. As a teacher, I find this simultaneously horrifying and encouraging. I grew up on the medium of print. I have been a voracious (if not always discriminating) reader from childhood to the present. My entire life has been greatly enriched by the practice of reading literature. I am also a lover of movies, which I have viewed with delight since childhood. Consequently I am afraid that these students are missing something important by settling for "one version"—whichever medium they have settled on.

At the same time, I am dazzled by the breadth of their viewing experience, the quickness with which they "read" film. That we are at (or already have passed) a point of change in the way we read and transmit cultural values and cultural experience is hardly a secret. Yet I remain convinced that by abandoning one medium for another, by abandoning earlier versions of any story for only one other version, we put ourselves at risk of losing a deeper historically based sense of who, as members of a given culture, we really are. And the crossover from medium to medium continues.

Where it was once common practice to adapt literature to the cinema, it is now nearly as common to find "novelizations" of successful movies or television series. The *Star Wars Trilogy* and *Star Trek* books come instantly to mind. More recently (1994), Louisa May Alcott's enduringly successful book, *Little Women*, was once again adapted for the big screen. The movie's release was followed by a spate of "new" novel-length books based on the characters in the Louisa May Alcott's original *Little Women*, releases timed to capitalize on the movie's theatrical release as well as on the continuing popularity of Alcott's book.[1]

The question of whether this profusion of media adaptations is a good thing or a bad thing matters less in the long run than the simple fact that, for good or ill, adaptation is here to stay. What matters most about each of these newly created and usually hybrid narratives (in film *and* in text) is that it satisfies the narrative appetite of its audience. Furthermore, however different the stories may be in some particulars, they are nonetheless related narratives sharing common material. Not surprisingly, this can (and often does) lead to some confusion.

---

[1]Two series of books in particular stand out. The *Portraits of Little Women* series, authored by Susan Beth Pfeffer, includes *Beth's Story, Amy's Story, Beth Makes Friends, Jo Makes a Friend, Meg Makes a Friend, A Gift for Meg, A Gift for Amy, Christmas Dreams,* and *Birthday Wishes*. The *Madam Alexander Little Women Journals* authored by Charlotte Emerson includes *Amy's True Prize, Beth's Snow Dancer,* and *Meg's Dearest Wish*, as well as number of harder to find titles.

In some instances, questions of "translation" or adaptation are simply that—problems in how to replicate in a given medium a story initially published in another.[2] Depending on the requirements of time, directorial vision, and budget, literary texts may be severely abridged and altered. In other circumstances, the literary underpinnings of a narrative may be almost invisible because they derive from textual material that has been metabolized by the culture at large to such an extent that it has become part of an invisible substratum of cultural knowledge. When this happens, the material resurfaces in various media as what have come to be considered stock figures, stock situations, and even in conventions of genre and form. The well-known fairy tale "Cinderella" offers a case in point.

My own first encounter with "Cinderella" occurred in 1947 or 1948. This involved not the Charles Perrault version on which the Disney animation was later based, but Fritz Kredel's translation of German folktales collected by Wilhelm and Jacob Grimm and initially published in 1812 under the title *Children's and Household Tales*. The story, as I first knew it, did not include a fairy godmother. Nor did it include step-sisters of the type exemplified by those in the Disney animation, who were as unattractive on the outside as they were greedy and cruel in their hearts. The Kredel translation *did* include a dead (but apparently good) mother and father so disengaged that, as a young reader with a different sort of father, I found him not particularly credible.

My own experience argued so compellingly against the possibility of a father

---

[2]As an example, consider Elia Kazan's 1955 *East of Eden*, a movie in which major characters and major plot elements (roughly 300 pages of the text of Steinbeck's novel) simply disappear, allowing the relationship between the brothers Cal and Aaron Trask to become not only the primary thematic concern of the story, but the *only* thematic concern. In this instance, the novel's complexity and much of its richness is lost. By contrast, Uli Edel's 1989 *Last Exit to Brooklyn*, which is remarkably faithful to Hubert Selby's novel of the same title, maintains the complexities of the book remarkably well and takes no real liberties with the development of theme until the movie's ending, at which time it very nearly destroys the impact of a movie that was, until the last sequence, both hard hitting and intelligent.

who would not notice the misery of his child that, even as a youngster, I saw Cinderella's father more as a narrative excuse for the events of the story than as a real character. Far more interesting to me than this distant and rather dull patriarch was the hazel twig sprouting from the grave of Cinderella's dead mother.

Today, the story in the Kredel translation seems to me less a pauper-to-princess tale than an intriguing overlay of earlier mythic elements.[3] For example, the heroine, Cinderella, achieves her success only with the help of a supernatural agent (her dead mother) rather than by her own efforts in the world, which would have been inappropriate female behavior, or even by the efforts of the man who should logically have been her protector, her father.[4]

When Cinderella's father departs on a journey, he asks all three girls, stepdaughters and true daughter alike, what he should bring back to them as a gift when he returns. The wicked step sisters request gifts of great material value, but the true daughter, Cinderella, asks only that he bring her the first twig to brush his hat when he journeys back home.

He brings her a hazel twig (a wand with fairly obvious sexual and magical connotations) which the true daughter then plants on her mother's grave and waters with tears. The twig becomes a tree. On its branches perches a white bird which can only represent the spirit of Cinderella's dead mother and which subsequently becomes the source of Cinderella's good fortune. This supernatural intervention makes possible the beleaugered young woman's trip to the ball where the prince will fall hopelessly in love with her, as a result of which he will ultimately make her his wife.

---

[3] In general, I think of fairy tales as stories lacking a specific time or place but related as actual fact. They differ from myth in some important ways–one is the specificity of mythic locations and times (as in the story of Oedipus) and the culture's understanding of mythic heroes as having had historical reality. Fairy tales also lack the culturally deep religious significance of myth.

[4] In truth, he is no such thing, describing Cinderella to the king's emissary as "only a daughter of my late wife's, a puny stunted drudge, but she cannot possibly be the bride" (Kredel 163)

The stepsisters, treated rather heavily in the Kredel translation, engage in bloody self-mutilation as they work to fit their feet into Cinderella's slipper. One cuts off a toe, the other a heel, both guided by their mother's advice that "when you are queen you will not have to walk any more"(162).[5] Neither is detected in this deception by the prince, who apparently cannot remember his sweetheart's face until the birds following him say "Prithee look back, prithee look back, / there's blood on the track . . ."(162). Later, at Cinderella's wedding to the prince, the stepsisters are walking side by side into the church when the birds fly down and peck out the outer eye of each.

After the wedding the stepsisters exit the church, still walking side by side but now with their direction reversed, so that their good eyes look outward. The birds peck out these eyes as well, so that the sisters are condemned to blindness, as well as to the crippling effect of their self-mutilation, for the rest of their days. Curiously, no mention is made of the fate of their mother. Cinderella's elevation to royalty, however, makes it shiningly clear that certain behaviors, in the long run, are ruinous to young women. Other behaviors are essential. While I will resist the temptation to draw the conclusion that the only good mother is a dead mother, I will point out that good mothering is a clear prerequisite in the female child's coming of age, and the "true mother" may make her power known from beyond the grave.

Yet this is not the "Cinderella" that most of the people I talk with today carry in the back of their heads—nor are any of the other pre-cinematic versions that I have encountered. The one that almost everyone thinks of first when asked to recall "Cinderella" is either the Disney animation or the Little Golden Book version of the story, a version derived from the Disney film.

---

[5]Unlike Cinderella's mother, who as she felt death approaching advised her child to "continue devout and good. Then God will always help you, and I will look down on you from heaven and watch over you" (155), this second wife is clearly invested in worldly advancement by whatever means necessary, caring nothing for her daughters' souls but a great deal for their social status. The contrast between the two mothers is crucial to the story's theme that mute goodness will gain a woman her best reward.

The popular concept of a "Cinderella story" is a curious admixture of Disney's rendering of the fairy tale and rags to riches tales such as *Pretty Woman*. In all of these stories, virtue is rewarded just as it is in the Kredel translation. Vice and vanity, of course, are not. In contrast to the brutality with which such failings are treated in Kredel's text, in the Disney animation they are dealt with bloodlessly.[6] In this fashion, presumably, the violent nature of punishment is kept entirely out of the script and there is nothing to mar Cinderella's complete if somewhat bland triumph.

Perhaps the most enduring figure created in this cinematic adaptation of the story is the fairy godmother—that plump and grandmotherly figure who has charmed so many of the audience for Disney's film (based on Charles Perrault's rendering of the fairy tale, initially published in 1697 in *Stories or Tales from Olden Times*, also known as *Tales of Mother Goose*). She is endearingly absent minded but powerful nonetheless and regales the audience with a bouncy patter song as she transforms poor Cinderella for her trip to the ball.

The extent to which the popular imagination has accepted this "fairy godmother" while letting go of the bird/spirit of the tale collected by the Brothers Grimm is remarkable. This fairy godmother has become a legitimate character in a variety of situations, surfacing again and again in popular fiction and in film. Indeed, the enabling fairy godmother has become institutionalized to such an extent that she not only gets Cinderella (in a variety of characterizations) over a rocky passage, but lets the audience escape from the barbs of its own conscience where uncomfortable social issues are concerned.

One example of this appears in *Pinky*, a "message" film released by Twentieth

---

[6]Another recent example of this "bloodlessness" occurs in James Finn Garner's *Politically Correct Bedtime Stories,* a parody in which "even the mother and sisters of step" (37) live happily ever after, all "womyn" having been redeemed by the development of comfortable clothing ("CinderWear") for their sex. That such a parody could be so widely read indicates, I suspect, a shift in our relation to at least some traditional fairy tales.

Century Fox in 1949[7]. The movie deliberately addresses specific racial issues—integration and miscegenation—that generated great cultural unease in the forties and fifties in America. Yet the movie is inevitably about other things as well, not least among them gender roles and the embedded coming-of-age narrative.

Pinky Johnson (Jeanne Crain) is an attractive young mulatto woman who has been in the north completing her nurse's training and passing for white. She has been wooed and all but won by a white doctor, Thomas Adams (William Lundigan). Pinky now returns home to visit her grandmother, Dicey Johnson (Ethel Waters).

Pinky's education, we learn, has been paid for by Dicey's hard-earned pennies. Pinky's purpose in this visit is to separate herself from her African American heritage, to say good bye. As the story develops, though, she realizes that this is not a simple decision. Against the security of love, marriage, and white identity she must weigh her inherited black identity and a community that has great need of her.

Should she abandon her grandmother and all her grandmother's labors, Pinky will become a stranger to her own past. Her grandmother, Dicey Johnson, is herself unfailingly resilient in the face of adversity, even when it includes the denial proposed by her granddaughter. Although Dicey condemns Pinky's wish to deny her own invisible blackness, she continues to love her grandchild without reservation.

Living next door to Dicey in a decaying but still impressive—one might even say looming—mansion, lives an aging white woman, Miss Em (Ethel Barrymore). At the outset, Pinky has nothing but contempt for Miss Em, perceiving her as the ultimate symbol of hypocrisy and racial oppression in the American south. She remembers that as a child she would stare longingly through the fence at Miss Em's garden and that Miss Em would never allow her to enter, in effect keeping her out

---

[7]Because *Cinderella* was not released until 1950, it is safe to assume that both the Disney production team and that of *Pinky* were influenced by the Charles Perrault version of the tale.

of the desired Eden.[8]

Pinky also points out that Miss Em's house itself is the product of slave labor. Yet the white and black older women are staunch friends, a circumstance that Pinky finds inexplicable. Dicey ekes out a living taking in wash and she wears her white friend's castoffs. Miss Em, who suffers from heart trouble, remains sequestered in her decaying mansion. The film's crisis emerges when Miss Em is stricken with a final illness and Pinky, against what she considers her better judgement, agrees to stay long enough to care for Miss Em until her death.

If we return for a moment to "Cinderella," certain similarities become clear. Both Cinderella and Pinky are bereft of their mothers. Both are deprived of fatherly protection. Cinderella's father scarcely notices her continued existence after his remarriage. Pinky's father is never mentioned, never even given an identity. Jake Walters (Frederick O'Neill), the black man who is supposed to be helping Dicey as she sends money to her grandchild in Boston, is in fact bilking her of almost everything.[9]

Both Cinderella and Pinky have participated in masquerades that have won them the protection of a "handsome prince," and both are stranded in the houses of hostile (step-)mothers. Miss Em's critical temperament and her asperity as she instructs her nurse to dust properly are not unlike the efforts of Cinderella's stepmother to demean the child of her husband's first wife. This is a great deal of similarity and deserves notice. While I am not trying to suggest that *Pinky* is "Cinderella" revised for 1949, I do want to make clear that *Pinky* is a story that relies heavily on the precedent of that fairy tale as it is understood in American popular

---

[8]This reference to the garden constitutes a challenge to the presentation in plantation fiction and its counterpart in film that the southern plantation was an Edenic site. For a fuller discussion of plantation tradition, see "History with Lightning."

[9]As a representative of patriarchal privilege, Jake Walters discredits both his race and his gender, a fact crucial to the film's enactment of what Thomas Cripps identifies as "shards of liberal conscience" (220).

culture.

Although *Pinky* is undeniably a film about race, this is a subject to which its approach is in some respects less than forthright. Pinky herself is, in every visual and auditory aspect, white. Nothing in the appearance, bearing, or speech of actress Jeanne Crain suggests that she was ever a member of an African American community. Admittedly, the film entertains the possibility that an educated black woman of good character can "rise above her station" if given the opportunity, but this rise entails a terrible cost, demanding that the woman who seeks to advance in mainstream society cast off much of the culture and community she came from.

In Pinky's case, the origins of opportunity lie in the paternalistic practices of the "Old South." Miss Em's house, with its looming presence and its forbidden garden, becomes her legacy to Pinky Johnson. This legacy is hotly contested in the local court, but upheld—in effect legitimized—by the white legal system which is also a part of Pinky's inheritance. Thus, at least in this particular movie, the white patriarchal institutions of the south are justified by the bequest of one of its spinster daughters to a light skinned mulatto.

This complex white legacy, not coincidentally, chases Pinky's suitor quite literally out of the picture. Thomas Adams, who urges Pinky to sell the house and come with him to start a new life where no one knows them, cannot compete with Miss Em's generosity. Even though it is decaying, the mansion has been placed (now that Miss Em has no further need of it) in the hands of an heir *of the slaves who built it*. Since the mansion has dominated the set all along, this outcome is not exactly a surprise. The descendant of slaves inherits the symbol of oppressive white power and is charged with turning it, at last, to some non-oppressive use, thereby fulfilling the moral requirements of the narrative.

Pinky, who was willing enough to deny her race when she felt herself a victim of oppression, is equally unwilling to pursue that course once she has independent means. Although the movie seems confident that the central issue for Pinky is moral and not economic in nature, it is very clear that economic self-sufficiency is a

94

necessary prerequisite to informed, free choice. While Pinky's suitor loyally wants to marry her despite the public notoriety her legacy has invited, he only wants the wedding to take place if she will repudiate what has become her *southern* inheritance (both white and black) to live with him where "there is no Pinky Johnson" (*Pinky*). If a viewer can manage to set aside the question of race, then the underlying Cinderella motif becomes much clearer.

Miss Em, whose death enables Pinky to achieve economic independence, is certainly something of a fairy godmother. But she is a godmother who frequently delivers her lines—she repeatedly instructs Pinky to be who she *really* is—with an acid tongue. Miss Em's grave may never be watered by her inheritor's tears (as in Kredel's translation from Grimm) and there are no snappy patter songs to entertain us, but the death of this old woman nonetheless makes it possible for the girl-becoming-woman to live in the castle. In an ironic turn, though, Pinky Johnson will be living in her castle as an independent woman rather than as a prince's bride.[10]

What then is one to make of Pinky's grandmother? Dicey who displays exemplary patience and dignity, who possesses the ability to rebound from crushing adversity, and who is both illiterate almost inarticulate when facing authority certainly needs to be considered if the movie's effort to confront racial stereotypes is be taken seriously. As the story comes to a close, Dicey becomes a grandmotherly presence, and determined laundress in what used to be Miss Em's house. Can we dismiss Pinky's original assessment of Miss Em's racial politics? The inescapable answer is that in these early days of the twenty-first century, we can't, in spite of the film's insistence that we do so.

Because of Pinky's appearance, there is an implicit suggestion that she is as much Miss Em's heir (at least in terms of social responsibility) as she is Dicey's.

---

[10]In this, *Pinky*, like the original fairy tales, uses property and status to keep the central female figure in her place. In the earlier tales, property accrued only to the male, and so the marriage was necessary to the female's well being. By 1949, women could and did hold property, and so Pinky was enabled to enact one of her story's great ironies, to *elevate* herself to a position of service.

What is crucial in the tension established by the film, is that neither of these women by herself commands sufficient maternal presence to usher Pinky successfully into adulthood. Both the tenderness and steadfast endurance of Dicey and the prestige and no-nonsense determination of Miss Em are necessary to prepare Pinky for her adult role.

Pinky's adult role is tremendously important in its own right, as it represents an attempt to resolve the questions raised by her story. Significantly, given the era in which the film was produced, Pinky must choose a role of service to the race. In the movie, this precludes any likelihood that Pinky herself will be producing children to inherit the legacy by which she herself has profited. Instead, she will nurse the children of others, presumably offering them an example of what is possible to the virtuous woman, even of black ancestry and even in the south.

Still, there is a financial bottom line that is disturbing. In the *Pinky's* world, even the whitest black cannot succeed without the backing of white money and white power. While the light-skinned Pinky may be a splendid nurse, she is still *only* a nurse, and must defer to doctors. This town's sole black doctor, who might be a suitable consort, is already married to someone else. He retains a degree of power based on gender as well as on professional status. While her inheritance represents a clear economic and even political gain for Pinky, it is also something of a dead end, locking her into a chaste life of service.

Pinky, as a social issues film, makes no claim to be based on the fairy tale that underlies so much of its story. A more recent and more clearly deliberate turn on the fairy tale motif emerges in *To Wong Foo, Thanks for Everything! Julie Newmar*. This is a movie that purports to be about gender, and although it certainly tackles that issue with enthusiasm, it is about other things as well. The presence of Wesley Snipes in a leading role guarantees a certain racial chic to the venture and the coming of age narrative remains central to the story. Like *Pinky*, *To Wong Foo* has absorbed the Cinderella tale and reshaped it to its own purposes.

The fairy godmother (or godmothers, to be more precise) are three drag queens: Vida Boheme (Patrick Swayze), Noxeema Jackson (Wesley Snipes), and Chi-Chi Rodriguez (John Leguizamo).

In *To Wong Foo 's* version of "Cinderella," the Cinderella figure is represented, at various times, by most of the important characters in the story as well as by some who are less notable:

- Vida Boheme is a drag queen whose mother lives in pseudo-Tudor splendor in Bala Cynwyd, Pennsylvania, whence she has banished Vida. This rejected daughter, like Cinderella, longs to take her place in the world but is denied the motherly aid and approval which would make that possible.

- Chi-Chi Rodriguez, a "sad little Latin boy in a dress" (*To Wong Foo, Thanks for Everything! Julie Newmar)* longs to be a drag queen but for most of the movie must settle for the status of "drag princess" *(To Wong Foo, Thanks for Everything! Julie Newmar*). She is mentored by Vida and Noxeema, who are co-winners of a drag competition and thus have become bona fide drag queens.

- Bobby Lee is a straight, small town, adolescent white girl, whose troubled parents (played by Stockard Channing and Arliss Howard) offer a far from reassuring portrait of marriage; Virgil is abusive and Carol Ann compliant; neither is happy. Bobby Lee nonetheless cherishes the conventional "Cinderella" dream of love and marriage and is in love with a fellow adolescent named Bobby Ray.

- Carol Ann, who is Bobby Lee's mother, is reduced by the nature of her marriage to the role of household drudge. She is a woman crushed by circumstance, unable to let her genuine beauty show as long as she is trapped in the kitchen cleaning up the mess where Virgil has flung the night's stew on the floor.

- Various residents of Snydersville who play relatively minor parts, but who are aided in their journeys to self realization by Vida, Noxeema, and Chi-Chi, also reflect the figure of Cinderella.

In addition to their roles as Cinderella, each of the drag queens also embodies the character of the fairy godmother—a deliberate social pun on which the film relies for much of its effect.

- Vida Boheme, as mentor to Chi-Chi, makes possible Chi-Chi's own victory as a drag queen. Vida is also responsible for Carol Ann's emergence from an oppressive marriage into personal fulfillment.
- Noxeema, in addition to mentoring Chi-Chi, assists the women of Snydersville in discovering their own beauty and "sense of style."
- Chi-Chi, despite her desire to beat most straight women at the games of fashion and romance, and despite her own infatuation with Bobby Ray, enables Bobby Lee to ensnare him and thus to achieve happiness.

Vida Boheme is the godmother-in-chief and most clearly nurturing of the three drag queens (or two queens and a princess). Revealed as Bala Cynwyd's rejected daughter, she is both racing *to* a competition in California and running *from* the pain that arises from her mother's refusal to acknowledge her. As the trio drives across the country en route to California, they are stopped by Sheriff Dollard for having a missing taillight. Vida is singled out for Dollard's unwelcome attentions. She pushes him away only to see him fall to the ground, apparently dead. Believing she has killed him, she flees, leaving on the highway a see-through plastic pump that is (forgive the pun) clearly a contemporary glass slipper.

It soon becomes clear that Dollard is not dead and that, shoe in hand, he is pursuing Vida. He believes that she is a dangerous pervert, in consequence of which the audience is made to understand that the prince (Dollard) is as much a representation of masculine authority as he is in the original tale. In this story, however, he is someone who must be evaded if Cinderella is to survive and triumph. In a pleasant variation on the original scheme, the shoe belongs not to Vida (the apparent Cinderella) but to the wistful drag princess, Chi-Chi. This is very logical since, according to her mentors, Chi-Chi doesn't know how to dress.

This would-be Latin drag queen, is first seen weeping on the steps of the drag competition where Vida and Noxeema have just been awarded the shared prize. The reason for Chi-Chi's distress is that she is not as beautiful as the two winners. Luckily for her, these two are not the wicked stepsisters of the Cinderella tradition. At Vida's urging, they "adopt" Chi-Chi and award her the status of "drag princess." In this role, Chi-Chi accrues princess points every time she does a significant deed indicative of what only be described as moral and spiritual growth.

Noxeema, as the only major African American character in the movie, is a more anomalous figure. Husky, clearly muscular even in her most outrageous outfits, her color makes her an outsider among outsiders. Noxeema is the one member of the trio who consistently counsels pragmatic common sense. She notes that "there are times when you help other people, and then there are times when helping other people will get you killed" (*To Wong Foo, Thanks for Everything! Julie Newmar*). It is worth noting, too, that the movie includes a long repressed interracial romance between local luncheonette owner Jimmy Joe[11] and one of the town's white women.

Subsequent to their encounter with the evil Sheriff Dollard, the three drag competitors are stranded by their apparently unfixable convertible in an unknown state in the small and poverty stricken rural town of Snydersville. They are effectively stuck in an area for which they have no map. Actually, the trio has driven right *off* the map and into the "once upon a time" limbo of fairy tales. They are able to literally transform the place with their nearly magical powers as drag queens.

Virgil and Carol Ann own the local hotel and gas station. Carol Ann is a

---

[11]In this nicely subdued episode of the film, the American cultural perception of the black man as in some degree feminized (See "Seeing in Black and White" for a fuller discussion of this) is treated as part of the Cinderella pattern. Like the women, Jimmy Joe comes to full self-realization through the agency of the godmothers. Also like the women, Jimmy Joe has been self-effacing, living a drab life providing a service no one really appreciates. In this, he reflects the cultural feminization of black males earlier evidenced by Jim in *Huck Finn*. In *Wong Foo*, the broad humor of the biologically masculine Noxeema as a fairy godmother is somewhat softened as a result of Jimmy Joe's emergence.

battered wife who will not admit to her suffering, preferring to weep in the kitchen and "put on a good face" in public. In this instance, Vida becomes Carol Ann's deliverer, vanquishing Virgil with a few strategically delivered punches and a great deal of righteous indignation. Carol Ann, in consequence, is transformed from kitchen drudge to fulfilled woman, resuming an active role in the town and recognizing that in spite of her years spent longing to escape from Snydersville, it is home. She is a Cinderella who renounces the castle for the hearth. She will remain in Snydersville and raise her daughters where they were born. But she will do it without Virgil, and with a strong sense of her own identity and importance.

When Sheriff Dollard finally arrives in Snydersville, shoe still literally in hand, it is the afternoon of the Strawberry Festival. Carol Ann, wearing what can only be described as a knockout of a red dress and swathed in a totally concealing red veil, now becomes Vida's deliverer. Carol Ann, who appears (in her ball gown) to *be* Vida, approaches Sheriff Dollard. He prepares himself to confront the ultimate evil he associates with drag queens only to find he is facing an ordinary housewife in a red dress. This anticlimax is fatal to the Sheriff's enterprise. With understandable anger, he leaves Snydersville, an action that Virgil imitates, wheeling his tow truck smartly down Main Street.

In her closing scene with Vida, Carol Ann both fixes the malfunctioning convertible and confesses the truth she has always known—that Vida is biologically male. She honors Vida's choice, however, by affirming how lucky she is to have a woman friend named Vida Boheme. When Carol Ann says "I love you, Vida Boheme" (*To Wong Foo, Thanks for Everything! Julie Newmar*), it is clearly a declaration of friendship, not of sexual passion or romantic love. Vida's response, "I have waited a lifetime to hear those words said to this name" (*To Wong Foo, Thanks for Everything! Julie Newmar*), provides at least one clear view of *Wong Foo*'s moral. Everyone must determine her own identity. That done, others must acknowledge and respect it. *Wong Foo* also insists that no one has to do this entirely alone and unsupported.

Chi-Chi's development is a case in point. Of the three self-proclaimed fairies, she is the most clearly and egregiously self serving. Her desires are happily superficial—a big house, vast closets of good looking clothes, and lots of attention. Its is no real surprise when, after she is nearly raped by the local "young toughs," Chi-Chi becomes an object of infatuation for her rescuer, young Bobby Ray, who is the object of Bobby Lee's adoration.

Chi-Chi, initially, is sufficiently hungry for attention that she sees no need to reveal the truth of her biological sex to Bobby Ray. She also sees no reason to consider Bobby Lee's feelings, even though the two have become friends. In a gesture that earns her the maximum possible number of princess points, Chi-Chi renounces her claim on Bobby Ray. We never know if she has told him the truth, but suspect that she has not. Still, her advice to Bobbie Lee is sound, as she tells the adolescent to "be honest with him" (*To Wong Foo, Thanks for Everything! Julie Newmar*). So it is that plain little Bobby Lee, transformed and dressed to the nines by three fairy godmothers, becomes attached to the local prince at the same time that one of the godmothers, Chi-Chi, becomes an adult in a world of nurturing women.

The rewards to Chi-Chi of her newly evidenced capacity for generosity show up in the movie's last scene when, replete with chic new hairdo, she is crowned the winner–a bona fide drag queen at last—in the California drag competition for which the trio was bound all along. The crown is bestowed on Chi-Chi by Miss Julie Newmar, who has been the "statuesque" talisman for Vida, Noxeema, and Chi-Chi since the beginning of their journey.

In *Pinky*, the fairy godmothers represented by Ethel Waters and Ethel Barrymore are embedded in the story so thoroughly that the nature of the fairy godmother figure is taken for granted and never fully explored. *To Wong Foo, Thanks for Everything! Julie Newmar*, on the other hand, requires its audience to engage and actually think about precisely that role.

By making of each significant female cast member both a Cinderella *and* a godmother, the film, which according to Roger Ebert is "as frothy as *Seven Brides for*

Seven Brothers" (1) works on a rather more serious level than Ebert seems to recognize. In his view, the movie is astonishingly "funny and amusing while tippy toeing around (a) sex, (b) controversy, and (c) any originality in the plot"(1). He concludes:

> It's amazing how entertaining it is in places, considering how amateurish the screenplay is and how awkwardly the elements of the story are cobbled together. I feel like recommending the performances, and suggesting they be ported over to another film. The actors emerge with glory, for attempting something very hard, and succeeding remarkably well. They deserve to be in a better movie. (1)

I suggest, to counter this view, that Ebert approaches the film from a perspective that is conditioned by film conventions, among them low-rent western sets, the notion (dispelled for all time, I would think, by *Pulp Fiction)* that ugly violence and comedy don't mix, the "buddy" aspect of the classic road movie, and even the Thunderbird convertible caught in Thelma and Louise's final freeze frame, forever in flight.

Admittedly, cinematic conventions form a crucial dimension of the movie, particularly the beat-up Cadillac convertible in which Vida, Noxeema and Chi-Chi drive (at least for while) not off the face of the earth but off the map and into a reality that is, for them, *terra incognita.* When Vida rips up and throws away her road map, she embarks on a journey that cannot be sufficiently read on a literal level. This brings me back again to my concern about those students (and others) who read the book or see the movie–but cannot be persuaded that there are greater riches to be gained if one does both.

What Ebert misses, or perhaps dismisses as too obvious to discuss, is that this particular film is a deliberate re-construction of the fairy tale. In this version, as in the Kredel translation (with its mutilated stepsisters), the violence (a battered wife, a malevolent sheriff, a scarcely averted rape) is the necessary subtext to the sunlit conclusion of a moral tale about identity. This is not to say that the moral direction of the tales is the same, but that the morals in both instances draw their meaning and strength from the terrible events that lie beneath the story's surface.

For the fairy tale Cinderella, identity was determined by the social conventions of her day. Because of her stepmother's opposition, this identity was achieved by the direct interference of the dead mother who in other versions was represented as a fairy godmother. For Pinky, whose role in life was somewhat modified by liberal social feeling, identity was also determined by the conventions of society at large. The intervening presences who made it possible for her to *claim* the identity that would allow scope to her talents and her training were the "fairy godmother" aspects of Dicey and Miss Em, whose real influence came into play only after Em had died. The uncomfortable implication that Em is, finally, the (god)mother who "counts," whose power, money, and influence really make things happen, is easily skirted in a fiction that insists on the indissoluble bond between the black and white figures of the two "godmotherly" women.

To Wong Foo, Thanks for Everything! Julie Newmar makes it clear that, at least in this 1995 film's construction, any woman should be able to define and claim her own identity. Furthermore, this identity should be, if not loved, accepted by all and respected by many. In a significant manipulation of the old story, the godmothers are all alive, exercise no supernatural powers, and contain within themselves the Cinderella waif.

Not surprisingly, all of them recognize that the violence and degradation implied by Sheriff Dollard and Virgil, as well as by Chi-Chi's would be rapists, is terrifyingly real. But it is not something they have to embrace or even to endorse. On some level, they can refuse engagement. If *that* aspect of their lives—the abused, degraded women they all might be—is allowed to triumph, then the moral purpose of the tale is lost. Thus, the violence is contained. The town of Snydersville is transformed.[12] Dollard and Virgil are banished. Young love has its triumph. When,

---

[12]The transformation of Snydersville is a melange of surface decoration (like adding beads to a woman's outfit, or draping bright table cloths on the dull, scarred tables of Jimmy Joe's luncheonette and the deeper transformation of attitudes as the women

at last, the (drag) queen wears the crown, there is no king with whom she must share it.

All of this suggests pretty strongly that the Cinderella narrative has been absorbed by American culture and recast in some rather startling ways. The old fairy tale now serves as what might be called a base-line narrative for a wide variety of situations in text and film. And certainly, Cinderella is not alone. The question of what actually happens as various stories make their way from print to celluloid is not an easy one to consider or to resolve. Duration of time is a factor that often dictates simplification of plot and character development. The point of view of a director is frequently at odds with that of the author of an earlier literary work. Audience response may vary simply because of the sensory channels utilized by these two very different media of expression. What remains absolutely clear, however, is that awareness of the pre-existent versions of any cultural narrative creates an audience far more alive to the richness of stories that are layered through cultural history and are not merely linear exercises in plot.

---

of the town (not the men, except for Jimmy Joe) come to feel, in the popular cliché, good about themselves for the first time. In an intriguing visual move, director Beeban Kidron echoes the scenes from Disney's Cinderella in which her animal friends (chiefly birds and mice) create a ball gown from scraps. In much the same way, Vida, Noxeema, and Chi-Chi transform their room in Snydersville from drab to glamorous.

Works Cited

Cripps, Thomas. *Making Movies Black.* New York: Oxford University Press, 1993.

Ebert, Roger. *"To Wong Foo, Thanks for Everything! Julie Newmar."* Compuserve. September, 1995.

Garner, James Finn. *Politically Correct Bedtime Stories.* New York: MacMillan, 1994.

Kredel, Fritz. Trans. *Fairy Tales of the Brothers Grimm.* New York: Grosset and Dunlap, 1945. 155-65.

Pinky. Dir. Elia Kazan. With Ethel Waters, Ethel Barrymore, Jeanne Crain, William Lundigan. Twentieth Century Fox. 1949.

To Wong Foo, Thanks for Everything! Julie Newmar. Dir. Beeban Kidron. With Patrick Swayze, Wesley Snipes, John Leguizamo. Universal. 1995.

Dead Already: Fathers and Anti-Feminism
in Three 1999 Films

In some ways, I'm dead already.

—Lester Burnham
American Beauty

I don't care what they say, this thing is broken.

—Lynn Sear
The Sixth Sense

He's not my father.

—Noelle De Angelo
Limbo

It is sometimes the case that a movie's apparent subject is not the element that it is, in some deeper sense, about. By about I do not mean "up to" precisely, but something very like it. In 1999, for example, we were treated to three movies that are, on the face of things, quite dissimilar: *American Beauty,* directed by Sam Mendes; *The Sixth Sense,* directed by M. Night Shyalaman; and *Limbo,* directed by John Sayles. The taglines supplied by the *Internet Movie Database* range from "look closer" (*American Beauty)* through "not every gift is a blessing," (*The Sixth Sense*) to the not very enlightening "a condition of unknowable outcome" (*Limbo).* A reasonable question at this point is what these movies have in common.

American Beauty is a grand evisceration of the sins of American suburbia. In this, it is a direct inheritor of movies like *The Graduate*. There is a comforting surface beauty, an illusion of orderly arrangement, to the upscale if ordinary suburban street introduced during the opening credits. The characters who populate this suburban arcadia, however, are for the most part frighteningly unbalanced, deeply out of touch with both their own needs and their obligations to consider the needs of others.

Using a proven sleight of hand (*Sunset Boulevard* comes to mind) the film is narrated by a central character who is already dead. The voiceover narration enlists the audience on the side of the speaker. Such is the power of this narrative trick that we do not question the ability of the dead to speak. Lester Burnham (Kevin Spacey) possesses a comfortably vernacular voice so knowingly snide in tone that we never associate the movie with the conventional thriller or horror genre. Despite the frequent interjection of Lester's rose-petal laden fantasies, the movie's presentation has a realistic feeling, probably because the frustrations of suburban homelife revealed in the plot are all too familiar to viewers.

The Sixth Sense, by contrast, *is* a thriller—the story of a little boy named Cole Sear (Haley Joel Osment) being raised in Philadelphia by his now single mother (Toni Collette). Cole's problem, aside from the lack of a father, is that he sees dead people. Although he is terrified by these visions, he knows that he cannot turn to his mother or his teachers for help. The movie is also the story of child psychologist Malcolm Crowe (Bruce Willis) who seeks to help Cole Sear come to terms with the things he sees and who, in helping Cole, must learn something about himself that he would rather not know.

That Malcolm Crowe must stand in the place of Cole's missing father is a given. Like *American Beauty, The Sixth Sense* is built around a central character who is dead. He appears to be participating as fully in the life of the living as Lester Burnham, though as the audience will later find out, he is not. Malcolm Crowe, as it turns out, doesn't know he is dead for most of the movie. He is not the narrator, but he shares with Lester Burnham (by his own admission already dead in some ways) a vernacular ease that combines with the frightening series of early events to distract the audience from any implications of Crowe's death.

Limbo, in a very different narrative mode, is the reflective tale of two divorced, middle-aged adults. Unemployed pulp mill worker Joe Gastineau and bar singer Donna De Angelo (David Strathairn and Mary Elizabeth Mastrantonio) seek a stable relationship with each other that will let them renew and sustain themselves. Their efforts to establish this relationship, already complicated by issues from their respective pasts, are most seriously threatened by De Angelo's pessimistic daughter Noelle (Vanessa Martinez). Like Cole Sear, Noelle must cope as best she can with her father's absence.

What all of these movies have in common, though it remains largely unremarked, is that each in its own way is preoccupied with fatherhood. Taken together, they form a poignant commentary on masculine anxiety about that beleaguered institution (all the fathers seem to be dead or missing in action) in the late nineteen-nineties. Each of these movies is haunted by a sort of hopeless nostalgia for dear old dad in which the viewer is asked to share, despite the father's lack of admirable qualities. In all three films, we are shown fathers and father figures who are in some measure lacking.

American Beauty, for instance, shows us Lester Burnham (Kevin Spacey) and Colonel Frank Fitts (Chris Cooper). Burnham is a suburban disaster—bright, articulate, college educated—trapped. Until his fatal but unremittingly cheerful rebellion, Burnham has no way to escape from a dead end job he loathes or from his marriage to a woman obsessed with their material possessions and her own loneliness. Like her husband, Carolyn Burnham (Annette Bening) does not see beyond the surface of things. The final soupçon of misery in Lester's life is provided by the apparently meaningless presence in his life of a sullen teenage daughter named Jane (Thora Birch) whose inner life is a complete mystery to her parents and to whom Lester himself is at best an embarrassment, as with his transparent lust for her best friend, and at worst a danger as he disregards her need for an engaged father.

The second of the movie's fathers is Colonel Frank Fitts. In contrast to Lester Burnham, he is a stiff spined, buzz cut, nearly over-the-hill military man who has taken up residence in the suburbs with his repressed, visibly unbalanced wife Barbara (Allison Janney) and his adolescent son Ricky (Wes Bentley). Ricky is already the veteran of a mental institution and a successful drug dealer. He is at various times brutalized by his father, who (if this is possible) is even more out of touch with the reality of his son's life than his neighbor Lester Burnham is with his daughter's.

While both the Burnham and the Fitts families are complete nuclear households—two parents plus offspring—both are tremendously dysfunctional. The real emotional "bang" of the movie is provided by Burnham and Fitts patriarchs and not by the other family members, who are incidental to the stories of the fathers, next to whom they seem to lack intensity and depth.

The Sixth Sense, pursuing a different narrative strategy, presents a single parent household. In this movie, mother Lynn Sear (Toni Collette) is left in Philadelphia to raise her young son Cole, an economic feat she manages by working two jobs while Cole's father resides in presumed bliss "in Pittsburgh with a lady who works in a toll booth" (*The Sixth Sense*). Lynn loves Cole and does everything in her power to help and protect him. She is a devoted and deeply committed mother. The demands of her two jobs (necessary because she supports Cole as well as herself) prevent her from being with her son as much as she would like. She cannot fathom his deepest secret and is badly frightened by the things that happen to him. Though far more engaged with her parental role, she is like the Burnham and Fitts parents in that she is excluded from the reality of her son's inner life.

In *Limbo* we see another single mother. Like the other parents mentioned so far, Donna De Angelo (Elizabeth Mastrantonio) does not know the reality of her child's life, which in this instance includes self-mutilation. She does, however, know that her daughter desperately longs for the presence and participation in her life of her father, a composer who has successfully ignored Noelle's existence for years. Lonely, independent, and often bewildered by the growing distance between herself and her daughter, Donna De Angelo has very few defenses against the world and the troubles it sends her way. She is, like Carolyn Burnham, visibly self-absorbed and somewhat brittle. She is likely to push too hard as she works to create new connections in her life and to improve her position with her daughter. Her growing relationship with Joe Gastineau seems, in some ways, like her last chance, but we are never shown how things actually work out.

As a father, *American Beauty's* Lester Burnham is a failure, something made clear by some of his daughter's lines. Two instances follow:

> To boyfriend Ricky Fitts:
>> I need a father who's a role model. Not some horny geek boy who's going to spray his shorts every time I bring a girlfriend home from school.
>>
>> *(American Beauty)*
>
> To her father:
>> You can't all of a sudden be my best friend just because you've had a bad day. You've barely spoken to me for months.
>>
>> *(American Beauty)*

Although both of these lines have a degree of adolescent smugness in their delivery, they nonetheless indicate Jane's awareness that something is wrong in her family circumstances.

As if to compound the distance that separates him from Jane, Lester embarks on a retrograde course of self-discovery, surrendering to his encompassing lust for Jane's friend Angela Hayes (Mena Suvari), a wannabe vamp who shares nymphets in general (and Nabokov's Lolita in particular) the potential to damage both herself and those around her as she moves towards her own identity. Lester, who is well within her sphere of influence, is a man desperate to find whatever quality made his youth such a good time for him. Lester, as his passion for Angela grows, begins working out, resumes smoking pot (conveniently supplied by the boy next door, Ricky Fitts), and uses blackmail to secure the severance package he wants after fourteen years as a self-described "whore" for the advertising industry. When Ricky Fitts suggests that the world of Lester's youth was fairly awful, Lester sets the record straight. "Actually," he explains, "it was great. All I did was party and get laid" (*American Beauty*).

Lester then attempts to recreate those years he remembers as having been so wonderful. Having secured a job in the fast food industry as a counterman at Mr. Smiley's (explaining that he wants "the least possible amount of authority" {*American Beauty*}), he purchases the car of his dreams—a 1970 Firebird. While all of this makes for an entertaining response to midlife angst, none of it can generally be described as adult behavior. Admittedly, Lester has secured a year's worth of salary and benefits that will prevent immediate financial disaster but this does not exonerate him from the charge of adolescent hedonism.

Colonel Frank Fitts, who occupies the house next door to the Burnhams, is also a father manqué, though he does not embark on a search for his vanished youthful zest. Like Lester Burnham, he is troubled by life and the world—though by different aspects of it. He is convinced that the nation and its citizens are in a serious decline, that homosexuality is shameful, and that people—particularly his son—must be closely watched. His most cherished possession is a piece of official state china from the Third Reich.

Unlike Lester Burnham, who tries to recover his vanished youth in a rash of self indulgences, Colonel Fitts finds the answer to life's perplexities in structure and discipline, qualities he believes can shape his own life and the lives of those close to him in such a way that those lives will be not only tenable but meaningful. For Fitts, this dedication to order is a nearly religious discipline, filled with articles of faith about structure, gender roles, and the sanctity of property. He violates Ricky's privacy and property continually in an effort to foster the virtues of structure and discipline.

Fitts is very distant from his wife. Mrs. Fitts, when not actively engaged in cooking or cleaning, retreats to a psychological inner state and merely occupies space in her own house. So complete is her withdrawal that she does not even hear people speaking to her. Ricky's withdrawal from the family takes another form. Having been caught smoking pot at an early age and having fought violently in school, he has been through the dislocating experience of living in a hospital where they "drugged me up and left me for two years" (*American Beauty*). All of this has occurred by the time he reaches his senior year of high school. Although Ricky Fitts does not hate his father and seems to want to some connection with him, he is also determined to live a life that his father despises. He deals and uses drugs and lies about both. He foils drug tests with the aid of a customer who supplies him with urine from the pediatric practice where she works. He counts on the power of his father's denial to help him pull it off.

Ricky Fitts refuses to fight his father physically and there is something of a desperate quality to his admission (while being beaten by his father) that he does need structure and discipline. His "Please Dad, don't give up on me" (*American Beauty*) could be taken for a sop to his father's authority were it not for Ricky's defense of his father to Jane: "He's not a bad man," (*American Beauty*) and his last request to his mother: "Take care of Dad" (*American Beauty*). Just before leaving home for good, Ricky endures another beating and an erroneous accusation of homosexual behavior. There is a terrible note of desolation when he looks at his father and says "What a sad old man you are" (*American Beauty*).

There is no serious question that both Jane and Ricky are in some measure damaged children.[1] Both of them *do* need structure and discipline. They need as well

---

[1]They are also shockingly glib and callous, at least to viewers who have arrived at middle age. When Jane dismisses her mother's melodramatic but real distress about her father's new career choice, refusing to participate in what she calls a "Kodak moment" (*American Beauty*) she is being both cruel and self-absorbed. Though the young are often both cruel and self-absorbed, age does not fully excuse her. As a balancing event, we have Ricky's farewell to his own father. When he dismisses his father as "a sad old man" (*American Beauty*), Ricky has both dignity and

to be protected from their own headlong rush to alienation. Both of them have mothers who are trying to fulfill expectations to which they are not well suited. Carolyn Burnham is trying to build a career (and a substantial income) in real estate sales; Barbara Fitts is trying to fill the shoes of the perfect homemaker. Carolyn, referring to her work's requirement that she be clearly and convincingly successful, insists: "Part of my job is to *live* that image" (*American Beauty*). She is really speaking for both herself and the nearly voiceless Barbara Fitts, who also narrowly skirts self-destruction as the two women attempt to live out images that are simply not true. That neither woman can see this about herself is chilling.

When Carolyn calls her daughter "an ungrateful little brat" (*American Beauty*), she is not entirely wrong. Inappropriate, yes. Self-absorbed, yes. Guilty of bad timing, yes. But she is not wrong. Jane Burnham is, in her way, as self-absorbed as her mother. Because Jane is an adolescent, we may think that she is *supposed* to be self-absorbed. Because Carolyn is an adult, we believe that she should not. Like many relationships, this one is shot through with contradictions and angers, grievances that neither party knows quite how to address, although it seems that Carolyn at least would like to address them in some fashion. Unfortunately, Carolyn's "fashion" has the appearance of cosmetic bandages, something in which Jane has no more interest than she does in anything else involving her parents.

Barbara Fitts, who cannot remember what her son will eat for breakfast, is not unlike Carolyn Burnham. Their styles may differ, but each woman is strikingly inappropriate in her maternal role. Barbara Fitts is unable to say anything relevant to her son when he leaves her house for the last time. Her sad advice that he should wear a coat indicates both her helplessness in the face of the emotional storm that has overtaken her family and a sorrowful wish that this might be the sage motherly expression that is called for. Both mothers, consumed by their own troubles, are

---

credibility–both of which are seriously strained when he sees the Lester Burnham dead in his own kitchen, and can only manage "Wow" (*American Beauty*).

disengaged from the present tense in which their children live. Neither is able to penetrate the salient facts about her child's existence. Neither knows how to make productive contact with the child she has brought into the world and who is now nearly grown.

To be fair, however, one must note that the children themselves repel their parents' interest. Ricky keeps his door locked. Jane plays her own life like a concealed poker hand, at least where her parents are concerned. Through their actions and their words, both Jane and Ricky indicate tremendous ambivalence about their parents, revealing contempt as well as the undercurrent of love that is sometimes perceptible to the viewer.

That one failed father should be killed by the other—who in the vernacular sense has "no life"—is not so terribly inappropriate. That the murder should center around misperceived homosexuality is bitterly ironic, but again, not terribly inappropriate. Once he has acknowledged his own willingness to "touch" another man—whether from his own lust or from a hunger for the son he has driven away—the only way Frank Fitts can possibly continue in this world is if he kills the only other person who knows of his lapse. That he may be avenging the imagined seduction of his son, or even on some level may be trying to understand that imagined seduction when he kisses Lester Burnham, does not mitigate his guilt, but it does help to make his anguish palpable. Unlike Lester Burnham, Frank Fitts is denied a happy ending.

Lester's death, though untimely, is astoundingly "happy" in the context of his life. Confronted with the fact of Angela Hayes' virginity, he has abandoned the long desired consummation of his fantasies and stepped back into fatherhood. He wraps Angela in a blanket. He reassures and comforts her. He fixes her food which is better received than anything prepared by Carolyn Burnham has been.[2] His last words,

---

[2] In an earlier scene in which he champions his own status as head of the household, Lester flings a serving dish of asparagus against the dining room wall (part of the Kodak moment Jane declined to share). By the movie's close, he is feeding a

114

"Man, oh man, oh man. . ." (*American Beauty*) are uttered in a tone of wonder as he contemplates a photo of his daughter. Ironically, he cannot do for his own daughter the acts of kindness he performs for Angela Hayes. He doesn't even know that Jane is preparing to leave his house forever with Ricky Fitts.

Alive, Lester Burnham would have to deal with the adulterous and bitter collapse of his marriage, the alienation of his daughter, his own attempted seduction of her best friend, his unwillingness to participate in the "adult world" and his equal reluctance to share his own views with Carolyn and Jane. Words shouted in anger—"They're *things!*" (*American Beauty*)—hardly constitute a helpful mode of discourse. Dead, he can look back on his life with gratitude, and (that narrative sleight of hand!) leave all of us feeling rather good about things despite the mess.

Also fatherless, though still young enough to be dependent on his mother, is Sear Cole, the eerily gifted little boy of *The Sixth Sense*. His mother, Lynn Sear (Toni Collette), however, is not quite up to the task of raising him. Working long hours, she has too little time to be with Cole as much as she would like and finds his actions baffling. Like Frank Fitts, she makes errors in assessing her son's behavior.

Unlike Frank Fitts, she has simple common sense on her side. When an object moves from place to place in the apartment and she knows she hasn't moved it, she assumes that Cole has. Unmoved by his denials, she remains ignorant of the active role played by ghosts in the life of her son. Curiously, she seems largely unaware of the fact that her life with Cole is also haunted by the ghost of her vanished husband, the man who by leaving them has also forced her more out of the household than she wants to be. The movie makes it clear that she can dispense love, but not understanding or insight beyond the very ordinary levels of reality. She says to her son, "I'm doing the best I can here . . ." (*The Sixth Sense*) but it is painfully obvious that her best isn't good enough.

---

surrogate daughter. While there is no overt claim in the movie that he is actually a better mother—or at least parent—than his wife, that is precisely what is implied in these two food serving incidents.

To some extent, the movie is dealing from a loaded deck. The circumstances of Cole's distress are *not* normal, nor are they readily accessible to anyone living in the real world as we know it. Thus, it doesn't matter how much Lynn loves her son or how hard she fights to protect him—she is denied the knowledge and experience that would let her in on his secret. In effect, it doesn't matter how good a mother she is; a different kind of intelligence, a *masculine* intelligence, is required to solve Cole's unusual problem.

Into Cole's troubled life comes Malcolm Crowe (Bruce Willis), child psychologist, who stands in a parental connection to his patients. He has, after all, received an award from the city of Philadelphia for "his continued efforts to improve the quality of life for countless children and their families" (*The Sixth Sense*). The wording of the award causes Crowe's wife to observe, in reverent tones, "They called you their son" (*The Sixth Sense)*. Crowe brings to the problem of Cole's visionary gift his superior education and past experience, perquisites of his gender and his social class to which Lynn Sear does not have access.

Like Cole, Malcolm Crowe is haunted, though not by the dead. In the movie's opening sequence, Crowe is confronted by Vincent Gray (Donnie Wahlberg), a former patient, now grown. Gray is overcome by rage and despair for which he blames Crowe's failure to treat him effectively. What he wants and needs is "what he [Malcolm Crowe] promised me" (*The Sixth Sense*). This is as much the nighttime cry of a troubled and terrified child as it is the accusation of a dissatisfied patient.

When Gray kills himself, the blame for that loss settles on Malcolm Crowe's shoulders. He will carry with him Gray's final accusation, "You were wrong. You failed me. Now look at me. I don't wanna be afraid no more" (*The Sixth Sense*) followed by "You failed me," and then again, screamed out *"You failed me!"* These are Gray's last words before his suicide and they supply the motivating guilt that Crowe carries with him into his relationship with Cole Sear. Cole, later in the film, will echo Gray by entreating Malcolm Crow: "Don't fail me!" (*The Sixth Sense*).

Crowe learns that Cole and Vincent Gray share a visionary gift. This gift has already destroyed Gray, and may destroy Cole Sear as well if Crowe does not manage Sear's case with consummate skill. Like Cole Sear, Vincent Gray had been a victim of divorce. Crow had in fact diagnosed the youthful Gray as having difficulty dealing with his parents' divorce. Now, the psychologist believes that by helping Cole he can atone for his failure with Vincent. In his efforts to do this, he encourages Cole to *listen* to what his visions have to say, to find out what they want of him. Significantly, the ghosts that actually speak to Cole for most of the movie are children. Of the two exceptions one is Malcolm Crowe, who is presented as a living participant in the story. The other is Cole's grandmother (Lynn's mother) who (unlike the other ghosts) never appears. Thus, the audience is made tremendously conscious of the dead children and the causes of their deaths.

One of these is a boy who has apparently been shot with his father's gun, an evidence of fatherly failure that the dead child doesn't seem to recognize.[3] This boy wants to show Cole where the gun is kept. The fact that much of the back of his head has been blown away seems, like his father's carelessness, not to concern (or even to have entered the awareness of) this adolescent ghost. Another youthful ghost, Kyra Collins (Mischa Barton), has a specific mission for Cole. He is to attend her wake, where he will go to her room, obtain a specific token, and give it to her father. Cole does this, giving to Mr. Collins (Greg Wood) a videotape of Mrs. Collins (Angelica Torn) poisoning Kyra. Thus is Mr. Collins, who now can protect his younger daughter, brought to an awareness of *his* duty as father.

Predictably, as Cole comes to terms with his gift, he must relinquish his connection with Malcolm Crowe. This means, among other things, that Crowe must accept his *own* death, the result of his having been shot by Vincent Gray just before Gray's suicide. Once Crowe accepts his own death, Cole can accept the loss of this surrogate father and be wholly truthful with his mother who, in spite of her reverence

---

[3]In this, the dead boy is like Vincent Gray and Cole Sear, who never indicate by their dialog that they are distressed by the loss of their fathers, although Cole provides at least one significant clue that this is the case.

for hard fact, is persuaded to believe him when he reveals that her dead mother, his grandmother, has been in touch with him and that she still loves Lynn Sear, who makes her proud "every day" (*The Sixth Sense*).

Like both *American Beauty* and *The Sixth Sense*, *Limbo* presents us with a damaged family. Bar singer Donna De Angelo (Elizabeth Mastranonio) is living in Port Henry (Juneau), Alaska with her teenaged daughter Noelle (Vanessa Martinez) for the duration of a booking at a local bar. For both, this is their first experience with the far north. They are dislocated and working to learn the rules of local life.

In her effort to "connect"—to make herself feel like part of something, Donna De Angelo has been living with a musician who is considerably younger than she is. Her method of severing the relationship reveals a self-absorption and desperation not unlike that of Carolyn Burnham. She is singing at a wedding reception where Noelle is working as a waitress. In the middle of a set, Donna seizes the opportunity to announce:

> This is my last appearance with Randy Mason and The Pipeline. I'll be continuing my run as a solo performer at the Golden Nugget while Randy will be sinking into the obscurity he so richly deserves. The time I have spent with him seemed much longer than it actually was.
>
> *Limbo*

She then sings a song of which the theme is that she is "better off without you in my life."

This breakup has the look and feel of an unpremeditated deed, an impulse the singer yields to on the spur of the moment. Randy Mason is obviously surprised, and Donna herself appears to be as well. Having announced in public that she is separating from Mason, Donna leaves the bandstand and bums a ride with Joe Gastineau, a stranger. Doing this, she leaves her daughter (who has witnessed the public scene) to find her own way home from work. The public nature of this breakup is necessary to Donna because it forces her not to reverse her decision, to live up to what she has declared. For Noelle it is a nightmare.

As we learn later, Randy Mason is one in a long succession of lovers. The transitory quality of these relationships makes it difficult, if not impossible, for Noelle to accept any one of her mother's boyfriends as a member of the household. Two abortive conversations make this clear. Donna offers an apology—" I'm sorry you got stuck at work. I just had to get out of there." Noelle responds "I'm used to gettin' home on my own. I just like to know where it is" (*Limbo*).

Referring to her mother's boyfriends, Noelle continues, "It's hard enough to keep their names straight. I'm supposed to like them?" (*Limbo*). When Donna responds "Don't *be* that way. I feel like shit. I could use a little support," Noelle is quick to reply "That's what therapy's for." Much later in the movie, when Donna is explaining what a nice guy Joe is, Noelle points out "They're all very nice right up until you say they're scum and shouldn't be allowed walking the streets" (*Limbo*). Noelle's not very subtle implication is that Donna needs a man—possibly any man—in her life, and has failed to choose any good ones.

Unable to adapt to the life that she has, Noelle clings passionately to a belief that her father, with whom she has never had any contact, really loves her.[4] Not knowing and not willing to try to understand how hard Donna has worked to compensate for the lack of a father, Noelle resists her mother's efforts at closeness with great energy. She both mistrusts her mother's judgement and blames her mother for the absence of the father she so longs for. When Donna begins dating Joe Gastineau the tension between mother and daughter becomes nearly unendurable.

Although Donna doesn't know it, Noelle is already acquainted with Joe from work and feels attracted to him. In an effort to resolve some of the discord and resentment between herself and her daughter, Donna agrees to take Noelle on a boat

---

[4]According to Donna, Noelle's father is "out of the picture—his choice" (*Limbo*), although Noelle prefers to believe that Donna dumped him before Noelle could be born. The truth, as the movie reveals it, is that all the Christmas gifts Noelle believes her father has sent were sent by her mother, who felt that (along with the Easter Bunny and Santa Claus) little Noelle should have "a father in California who sent her presents" (*Limbo*).

trip up the coast with Joe and his half-brother Bobby (Casey Siemaszko), a choice she might have avoided if she had known of Noelle's interest in Joe.

Up to this point, there is a rather wistful quality to the relationship between Joe Gastineau and Donna De Angelo. Joe has been married and both have had other lovers. Both long for something more solid, but are not sure even that such a thing is possible. And there is the daunting difficulty of winning Noelle to such a project. Certainly, her mother hopes that the boat trip will help. Unfortunately, Joe's half-brother has (without Joe's knowledge) gotten involved in a drug deal, and owes some people more money than he can possibly pay. The net result of this is the murder of Bobby Gastineau and the destruction of his boat. Joe, Donna, and Noelle are able to escape to an uninhabited island where, cold and with no supplies, they must survive until help comes. The environment is so hostile that they know they cannot come through the impending winter there. They have no workable means of escape.

During their stay on the island the three discover a ruined house, the abandoned home of a family that had hoped to create a life there, though they apparently failed. This does not seem to bode well for the new residents, whose chief occupation is keeping a smudge fire burning on the beach in the hope that they will be spotted. This may be a wise or a foolish hope, depending on the viewer's perspective, since there is no reason to believe that anyone will be looking for them in that remote location.

The three survivors are generally cold, undernourished, and frequently uncomfortable with one another. Noelle finds any signs of sexual intimacy between her mother and Joe distressing. In the house, Noelle finds the diary of Ann Marie Hoak, the daughter of the family whose homestead they have found. From this diary she reads a little aloud each night. In truth, only the first few pages of the diary contain any writing—the rest is a fiction Noelle creates each evening for the two adults.

But Noelle is not a Sheherezade who spins fanciful entertainments to prolong her life. The tale Noelle unfolds reveals her deep depression and alienation, cast as the personal diary of young Ann Marie Hoak. For Ann Marie, Noelle imagines a suicidal mother and a father whose physical ailments prevent him from working at trades available within the town of Port Henry. She also creates for the Hoak family a fox farming venture in which at least one of the vixens eats her young. The story Noelle tells is a story of abandonment and despair which, to her credit, Donna repudiates, insisting that she would never abandon her daughter, not even by dying.

The most obvious question posed by the trio's situation is whether these people—any of them—will survive. By the movie's close it is clear that they must *all* live or *all* die. Because they are taking care of each other, and because they are marooned, they seem to be forming a family unit. They are not always easy together, but out of necessity each is committed to the group. Whether they can actually form a family remains an open question. Noelle is depressed and resentful. Donna pushes too hard in her efforts to connect with her daughter. Not until Noelle falls ill, something that happens only *after* she has learned that her father never sent the gifts she believed came from him, will she let her mother hold her.

Despite his responsible nature, Joe Gastineau is the interloper here. It is largely his fault they are in this situation. As Noelle is happy to point out while they hope for rescue, "I shouldn't be here. I shouldn't be in this state" (*Limbo*), a sentence that encompasses both her geographical dislocation and her psychological condition. When Donna appeals to Joe—"You could help me with this" (*Limbo*)—Noelle's immediate response is "He's not my father" (*Limbo*). Yet Joe, although he did get the two women into their current mess, is also the reason that they are still alive.

By making the best of terrible circumstances, by feeding their smudge fire, by trapping fish, and so on, all three of the castaways are responding to the exceptional pressure of their isolated situation. It is anyone's guess whether this complex three way relationship will continue to develop if they get back to the mainland.

Director John Sayles denies us a resolution. Eventually, the signal fire tended by the castaways is seen and Smilin' Jack (Kris Kristofferson) brings his small plane in. Jack is at best an ambiguous figure—likeable, but untrustworthy—known equally for his tenacity and for his willingness to deal on the wrong side of the law. Where Donna and Noelle see a rescuer, Joe sees a threat. When asked, Jack admits to Joe that he was hired by strangers "Mr. Smith and Mr. Brown" *(Limbo)* to find the three castaways and report their whereabouts. Yet he leaves them his first aid kit and promises to return.

Like the castaways themselves, the audience wonders if Jack can be trusted. Like the castaways, the audience finds no sure answer. When a plane returns, the three who are waiting with their terrible burden of hope and suspicion linger in the tree line at the edge of the beach. The first to step forward is Donna, who simply says "The hell with it. I won't stay here" *(Limbo)*. Noelle comes forward, and stands with her mother. The last to come forward is Joe Gastineau, the man who knows that "you can't always save people" *(Limbo)*, who finally joins the mother and daughter on the beach, completing what might yet become a family. The three are holding each other, looking at an extremely uncertain future, when the point of view switches. The audience is looking through the windshield of the plane at the small shingle of beach when the view goes black and the credits roll.

The fate of Donna and Noelle De Angelo and of Joe Gastineau remains uncertain. It is impossible to ignore the ambiguity of their final stance. Unlike the Fitts and Burnham families, they are not hopelessly divided, and unlike the situation for Cole Sear, there is a living man present who is willing to fill the role of father, though his ability has yet to be fully tested. Despite the unhappy fact that these individuals have all been damaged by life, as a group they offer some hope in what can best be described as an unhopeful situation[5].

---

[5]A decidedly grimmer scenario, reflecting similar discomfort, is proposed by the 1999 Canadian film, *The Highwayman*, directed by Keoni Waxman. This movie, shifts things around a bit. We are presented not with a damaged family, but with no family at all. The protagonist, Ziggy, is a young woman on her own. Desperate to find the father she has never known, apparently having no mother, she has only her boyfriend as an emotional anchor throughout her quest and she doesn't seem to like hm very much She is drawn to the excitement and danger, and to the possibilities of new

122

What does all this add up to? All three of these films direct longing and outrage at fathers, and all three denigrate mothers, perhaps not such a curious strategy in the wake of *Iron John* and the Million Man March. In *American Beauty,* Carolyn Burnham and Barbara Fitts are both hopelessly out of touch with their children's lives and also with their own complicity in accepting social roles to which they are ill suited. *The Sixth Sense*'s Lynn Sear, who is a *good* mother, hasn't got a clue to what her child is going through while Mrs. Collins copes with her personal demons by murdering her daughter. In *Limbo,* Donna De Angelo is too embroiled in her own problems (one of which is her distant daughter) to enter into the girl's life on a useful level. Only when mother and daughter are removed altogether from the social frame do the pair begin to address the deep divisions between them.

The children in these movies, moreover, are pretty desperate for effective fathers and know it. Jane Burnham observes about her father's obsession with Angela Hayes: "It would be nice if I was that important to him" (*American Beauty*). Cole Sear wears his father's watch—which is broken and which his father forgot when he left—with such apparent devotion that Malcolm Crowe thinks his father must have presented it as a gift. Cole does not encourage this misapprehension. "He forgot it in a drawer. It doesn't work" (*The Sixth Sense*).

While we do not see Cole express any anger at his father, we know that he understands his situation (and his mother's) to be that of things forgotten, things that (most likely) don't even work. And we *do* see Vincent Gray's anguished fury at Malcolm Crowe, who stands in an emotionally paternal relation to him. Noelle De

---

things represented by a pair of armed robbers with whom she hooks up. These two bear the unlikely names of Breakfast (Jason Priestley) and Panda (Bernie Coulson). It can hardly be accidental that these names echo of childhood security in the form of a morning meal and stuffed animals, but this is a remarkably sardonic echo given their occupation (armed robbery), and their personalities (which are violent in the extreme), and their propensity fo act on whim. Although Ziggy *thinks* she has found her father, the man was in prison at the time of her conception (apparently without conjuagal visits). Even this doesn't dissuade her from her conviction that he is her Dad. Ultimately, fatherhood becomes a question of mistaken identity and confused emotional responses, a fiction with no counterpart in the movie's "real" world.

Angelo, in *Limbo*, longs for her father with a desperation almost too painful to watch, and is nearly destroyed by the knowledge of his indifference to her. Whether she will be able accept a substitute is one the movie's great questions.

When Karen Hollinger noted in her *In the Company of Women* that there had been, by 1998, remarkably little in the way of backlash against the feminist road and buddy movies of the eighties and early nineties, she may have been speaking just a little too soon. To be sure, these three movies are not the sort of backlash that fueled *The Hand that Rocks the Cradle*. In that instance, the audience was confronted with the story of a wife and new mother, Clair Bartel (Annabella Sciorra), who desires to use her talents outside of the home. She hires a nanny, Peyton Flanders (Rebecca de Mornay), who turns out to be evil incarnate. Peyton's propensity for human destruction exists, we are told, because her own maternal nature has been thwarted. The subtext of the movie, rather obviously, is that women should stay put at home and that the men should see to it.

That is not the case presented by these movies from 1999. Admittedly, Donna De Angelo, Carolyn Burnham, and Lynn Sear do, in fact, work outside the home. What sets them apart from Claire Bartel is that they *need* to work outside the home (or at least believe that they do) because their husbands are not satisfying the family's needs. Barbara Fitts, who *does* stay home, is crazy. So is Mrs. Collins, who murders her daughter for reasons that are never disclosed. Generally, domestic space doesn't look like a very good location for a woman.

In Carolyn Burnham we see a woman who is obsessed with material possessions because she believes they will either fill her empty life or compensate for her misery. As a realtor, she spends her life with empty houses which she can apparently clean very well but cannot sell to anyone, a fact that triggers her deep despair. Perhaps the saddest fact about Carolyn's desires is that they are so ordinary—she is, after all, still in suburbia. Her daughter is in public school. Her husband (at the outset) drives a Camry. None of this is very impressive, despite the "$4,000.00 sofa" (*American Beauty)* in the Burnham front parlor. Housewife Barbara

Fitts, as already noted, is crazy. Like Carolyn she cleans magnificently but cannot make the home a safe haven. Lynn Sear, despite her two jobs, is visually presented in terms of domestic space (the explosion of laundry in the apartment, the rush of getting Cole a breakfast before she goes to work, fantasizing that she has quit her jobs). That she cannot manage her domestic space better is the fault of her employment, which she cannot give up and still maintain the home at all. Mrs. Collins, a homemaker, murders her child. Donna DeAngelo tries over and over to create something like normal, nuclear family domesticity, and fails.

Carolyn Burnham, of course, doesn't kill her child, though her relation to domestic space is not particularly good. Instead, Carolyn gets *her* biggest bang firing a pistol on a target range. This looks, in symbolic terms, like a wistful usurpation of phallic power, a usurpation facilitated by her lover, Buddy Kane (Peter Gallagher), who is as shallow as she is. Carolyn's husband Lester, who very much wants traditional, adult male prerogatives (not to be interrupted, not to be told what to do, a voice in music selection at dinner . . .), is so busy pursuing his lost youth that there is no reason to think he deserves them. Carolyn's neighborhood counterpart, Barbara Fitts, is a somewhat different case, having withdrawn from her home without having left it. Living in her own interior spaces, she is no better a mother than Carolyn Burnham.

Lynn Sear and Donna De Angelo, very obviously, *do* have to work—their men have not only opted out of their lives, but have taken new women as mates and do not contribute to the welfare of Cole and Noelle. Both of these women project a savvy, tough exterior, and both know the rules of the game in their economic segments of American society. Both have children who long deeply for missing fathers. Even Jane Burnham longs for her father, who is missing in a way she can't define.

The central problem of both the women and the children in these movies has to do with the makeup of the nuclear family and the difficulty of replacing a missing member. Carolyn Burnham tries taking a lover, Buddy Kane, who leaves her flat when their affair is discovered. Barbara Fitts, perhaps not even knowing what she lacks, simply withdraws. Lynn Sear tries to tough it out alone, but is unable to make sense of her son's difficulties. Donna De Angelo goes from relationship to relationship, always hopeful and always disappointed, until she teams up with Joe Gastineau. How that will end is anybody's guess, but it is perhaps a telling detail that Joe is the last to step onto the beach of commitment with Donna and Noelle.

All of these families (or family-shaped units) are in desperate shape, but most desperate, in an odd way is the father. As Lester Burnham so artfully puts it at the beginning of *American Beauty,* "In some ways, I'm dead already." Malcolm Crowe is dead and doesn't even know it. There is no living man whom Cole Sear can trust. To Noelle De Angelo and to Cole Sear, their fathers *are* dead. All their love and longing will not bring about a reunion any more than if these men were actually six feet under. Whether Joe Gastineau can step into fatherhood is unknown, and whether Lester Burnham's burst of fatherly emotion for Angela Hayes actually redeems him is a moot point.

In an earlier generation of movies that attacked American family life, the convention was to look to the children for hope. In the present generation of films that is not a reliable option. Jane Burnham, who does have problems, is sullenly self-absorbed, worried not about *life,* or *the meaning and purpose of life,* but about the level of emotional comfort in her *own* life. Noelle De Angelo, though more deeply troubled, is not all that different.

Cole Sear, who is much younger and who shows no signs of the sexual ambivalence present in the girls, deals with the dead better than with his father. At least the dead will talk to him. Ricky Fitts, voyeuristic observer of everything and amateur filmmaker, is not much help, as he may or may not be seeing things any more clearly than those who surround him. *His* response to life is to head for New York and a career dealing drugs. His symbol of what he thinks is the joyous beautiful life that exists beneath the surface of things is an empty bag blown by the wind. Despite his eye for beauty, he is drawn to emptiness—a dead homeless woman, a dead bird, the empty husk that is Lester Burnham's body.

So it looks, after all, as if Dad has withdrawn from the family struggle and taken the whole mess down with him. The women, even when they are strong and good, are not fully adequate as parents to meet their children's needs. The children themselves aren't clear on much except that their lives are somehow very screwed up. With the possible exception of Cole Sear, they are not especially nice people. Nor are they clear seers of the world.

So we are left. Noelle De Angelo stands between her mother and her mother's boyfriend, still carrying the weight of her father's defection. Ricky Fitts looks at the dead face of his girl friend's dad and says "Wow!" (*American Beauty*), more at one with the esthetic moment than concerned about who might have committed this murder or why. Jane Burnham looks into the bloody kitchen and forlornly mumbles "Dad?" (*American Beauty*) Carolyn Burnham hides her own gun in a hamper, keens, and hugs her husband's empty shirts. Her transcendent emotion is tremendous, shocking grief. Cole Sear has said his sentimental farewell to Malcolm Crowe's ghost—the one ghost who reached across from the other side and consistently helped him[6].

All the children are, in very real terms, fatherless. They are not coping as well as one might hope. Noelle, not at all sure what will happen, must balance the weight of her mother's betrayal with the weight of her love, must decide whether to accept Joe Gastineau. Ricky Fitts must make his way in the world, knowing that his father will not even look for him. Jane Burnham, spoiled and self-absorbed, must finally face an inescapably *real* event in her family's history. Cole Sear has his mother, a world of ghosts, and a broken watch. Effectively, he is bound into a world of women.

Donna DeAngelo is still pushing too hard, unable to weigh consequences.

---

[6]Although his grandmother visited him and kept putting his mother's treasured brooch in Cole's drawer, this created more stress for the child. Far from comforting him, it landed him in trouble with his mother–serving as yet another example of the ineffectiveness of even the best-intentioned women. Also, when Cole finally makes his gift known to his mother he does so by delivering a message–like the other, younger ghosts, his grandmother seems to have come to him for help.

Barbara Fitts is simply lost—left behind to "take care of Dad" (*American Beauty*) but likely not to do so very well. Carolyn Burnham is absorbed in loss. Lynn Sear has a son who will finally talk to her, but whose world is never going to be the one she lives in, the one she can understand.

As different from each other as these movies are, ranging in genre from thriller to survival adventure to suburban dark comedy, all of them are built on the foundation of fatherhood gone awry. Fathers may not come off terribly well in these movies, but they are the most crucially important figures in them. Lester Burnham and Frank Fitts, by *American Beauty's* end, are the only characters about whom we can actually care. So, to a lesser extent, is Joe Gastineau, though Noelle's judgmental, "He's not my father," haunts the final tableau. Her real father is in California. He's a composer. She doesn't even know him. Mr. Sear is in Pittsburgh and the admirable Malcolm Crowe has left the theater to enter another realm. At the last, each father is both blamed and absolved, absurdly loved and absurdly absent as these movies dramatize their bitter fantasy:

You'll be sorry when I'm gone.

Works Cited

American Beauty. Dir. Sam Mendes. With Kevin Spacey, Annette Bening, Thora Birch, Wes Bentley, Mena Suvari. Dream Works. 1999.

The Hand that Rocks the Cradle. Dir. Curtis Hanson. With Annabella Sciorra, Rebecca de Mornay, Ernie Hudson. Hollywood Pictures. 1992.

The Highwayman. Dir. Keoni Waxman. With Bernie Coulson, Louis Gosset Jr., Laura Harris (II), Stephen McHattie, Jason Priestley. Lions Gate Films/ Sterling Home Entertainment. 1999.

Limbo. Dir. John Sayles. With Mary Elizabeth Mastrantonio, David Strathairn, Kris Kristofferson, Casey Siemaszko. Green/Renzi. 1999.

The Sixth Sense. Dir. M. Night Shyalaman.With Bruce Willis, Haley Joel Osment, Toni Collette. Hollywood Pictures/ Spyglass Entertainment. 1999.

Index

Adventures of Huckleberry Finn (The) 4, 12, 23, 17, 27
    Aunt Polly 5, 39
    family 13, 14, 17, 23, 25
    Huck 12-18, 20, 24, 25, 30, 38, 77
    Jim 12-15, 17, 18, 20, 23-25
    Pap 13
    Sheperdson-Grangerford 13, 38
    Tom Sawyer 13
Aja, Alexandre 5
    Alexander Arkady 5
    Furia 5
American Beauty .... ii, 105-107, 109-111, 116, 122, 123, 125
    Carolyn Burnham 107, 123, 124
    Lester Burnham 106-111, 113, 114, 125, 127
    Allison Janney 108
    Angela 109
    Angela Hayes 109, 113, 114, 122, 125
    Annette Bening 107
    Barbara Fitts 108, 112, 122-124, 126
    Chris Cooper 107
    Colonel Frank Fitts 107, 108, 110, 113, 114, 127
    Jane 107
    Jane Burnham 109, 111-114, 122, 124-126
    Kevin Spacey 106
    Mena Suvari 109
    Ricky Fitts 108, 111-114, 125, 126
    Sam Mendes 105
    Thora Birch 107
    Wes Bentley 108
American narratives 14
Baudrillard 5
Being There 44
    Chance (Chauncy Gardner) 44
    Hal Ashby 43
Bordwell, David 1
Brent, Linda (See also Harriet Jacobs) 28
Birth of a Nation (The) .... ii, 4, 47-58, 60, 61, 63, 64
    Aitkin Spottiswoode 49
    Austin Stoneman 49
    Ben 51
    Ben 49
    crosscutting 48
    Dr. Cameron 49
    Duke 49
    Elmer Clifton 49
    Elsie 49, 51, 54
    Flora 50-52
    George Beranger 49
    George Siegmann 50
    Gus 50, 52, 54, 62

130

Henry B.Walthall 49
historical facsimile 60
Josephine Crowell 49
Lillian Gish 49
Lydia Brown 49, 62
Mae Marsh 50
Margaret Cameron 49
Mary Alden 49
Maxfield Stanley 49, 50
Miriam Cooper 49
Ralph Lewis 49
Phil Stoneman 49
Robert Harron 49
Silas Lynch 50
Thaddeus Stevens 49
title cards 54, 58, 59, 62
Tod Stoneman 49
Wade Cameron 49
Brother from Another Planet (The) 4, 27
A-Train 32
abolitionism 33
Card Trickster 32
David Strathairn 37
Ellis Island 35
Harlem 32
Joe Morton 35
John Sayles 37
Men in Black 37
The Brother 34
Virgil 35
Butch Cassidy 5
Butch Cassidy and the Sundance Kid 69, 71, 74
Brian May's 5
Brooks, Van Wyck 39
Brothers Grimm ii
Calamity Jane 77
Calvin and Hobbes . . . . ii, 4
Bill Watterson 10
black and white 11
Calvin . . . . iii, 10, 11, 18
Calvin's father 11
comic strip 11
Watterson 10
Captivity narrative 73-76, 79, 81
Dustan 75-77
Rowlandson 74-77, 79
Casablanca 1
Cinderella 87-90
Charles Perrault 87, 90
Cinderella story 90
Fritz Kredel 90, 94, 101
Disney 87, 89, 90, 102

Wilhelm and Jacob Grimm 87, 90, 94
Citizen Kane 1
Civil War 27, 47-50, 52, 56-58
Clemens, Samuel (See also Mark Twain) 4
Colonial America 10
Cooper, James Fenimore .... ii, 4, 12, 23, 24, 30
    Chingachcook .... ii, 12
    Leatherstocking Tales 20
    Natty Bumppo 12, 77
    Leatherstocking Tales 20
    The Pioneers 23
Cripps, Thomas 16, 92
    Making Movies Black 16
Defiant Ones (The) 4, 15
    Joker Jackson 15, 16
    Noah Cullen 15, 16, 24
    Sidney Poitier 15
    Stanley Kramer 15
    Tony Curtis 15, 16
Die Hard 4, 16, 19
    Al Powell 19, 20, 24
    Alan Rickman 19
    Bonnie Bedelia 19
    Bruce Willis 19
    Hans 19
    John McClane 19, 20
    John McTiernan 19
Dixon, Thomas 47, 49, 53, 55-57, 60-64
    The Clansman: An Historical Romance of the Ku Klux Klan 47, 56
    The Traitor: A Story of the Rise and Fall of the Invisible Empire 56
    The Leopard's Spots: A Romance of the White Man's Burden 56
Douglass, Frederick 14, 31
    Garrison, William Lloyd 31
    Narrative of the Life of Frederick Douglass 28
Drum 52
Ebert, Roger 78, 80, 81, 100, 101
Fairy godmother 87, 90, 94-98, 100-102
Fairy tale 78-81
Franklin, John Hope 55-58, 61
gender. 4, 70, 71, 74, 75, 77, 81
genre 71, 78, 81
Goldman, William iii
Gone With the Wind 52
Graduate (The) 106
Green Mile (The) .... ii, 4, 19, 20, 24
    black sexuality 22
    Castle Rock Films 19
    Christ Figure 21, 23
    Doug Hutchinson 21
    Frank Darabont 19, 20
    Fred Astaire/Ginger Rogers 23
    Gary Sinese 21

132

John Coffey 19, 21, 22, 23
John Hammersmith 21
Michael Duncan 21
Paul Edgecomb 21, 22, 23
Percy Wetmore 21
Sam Rockwell 21
Tom Hanks 21
William "Wild Bill" Morton 21
Griffith, D.W 4, 47, 48, 53-56, 62, 63
Guerrero, Ed 52
Highwayman (The) 121
Bernie Coulson 121
Breakfast 121
Jason Priestley 121
Keoni Waxman 121
Panda 121
Ziggy 121
Hill, George Roy iii
Jacobs (Harriet) 14, 28
Incidents in the Life of a Slave Girl 28
Johnson, Jeremiah 77
Johnson, Richard 68
Ku Klux Klan 47, 48, 51, 52, 59, 61, 62
Leatherstocking Tales 4
Leaving Normal 5, 67, 72, 77, 78, 80, 81
Darly 79-81
Marianne 77-81
Cece 78, 79
Darly 77
Meg Tilly 77
Patrika Darbo 78
Lethal Weapon .... ii, 4, 16, 17
Danny Glover 17
Hunsacker 17
Martin Riggs 17
Mel Gibson 17
Murtaugh 17-19, 24
Richard Donner 17
Riggs 17, 18, 20, 21
Roger Murtaugh 17
Warner Brothers 16
Limbo .... ii, 5, 105
Ann Marie Hoak 119
Bobby 118, 119
Casey Siemaszko 118
David Strathairn 107
Donna 123
Donna De Angelo 107, 109, 116-118, 122-124
Hoak 119
Jack 121
Joe 121
Joe Gastineau 107, 109, 117, 118, 120, 121, 124-127

    John Sayles 105, 120
    Kathryn Grody 107
    Kris Kristofferson 120
    Limbo 105, 116-118, 120-122
    Mary Elizabeth Mastroantonio 107
    Noelle 107, 117-122, 124-127
    Noelle 121
    Randy 117
    Randy Mason 117
    Smilin' Jack 120
Mandingo 52
Mintz, Steven 1
Mulatto 49, 54
NAACP 55, 62
Olney, James 30
Page, Walter Hines 56
Pfeil, Fred 19
    White Guys 19
Pinky 5, 90, 92-95, 100
    coming-of-age narrative 91
    Jeanne Crain 91-93
    Dicey 91
    Dicey Johnson 91, 92, 94, 102
    Ethel Barrymore 91, 100
    Ethel Waters 91, 100
    Frederick O'Neill 92
    Jake Walters 92
    miscegenation 90
    Miss Em 91-94, 102
    Pinky Johnson 91, 93-95, 101
Plantation fiction 53, 54, 57
    stereotypes 53
Plantation tradition in film 52
Race 4, 19, 18, 21, 22, 25, 27
Reconstruction 47, 48, 50, 56-58
Roberts, Randy 1
Rosenblatt, Roger 30
Rowlandson, Mary White 5
Sayles, John 4, 27
Sayre, Robert F 30
Schickel, Richard 1, 72
Sixth Sense (The) 5, 105, 106, 108, 114-116, 122
    Bruce Willis 106
    Cole Sear 106, 115, 116, 121, 122, 125, 126
    Haley Joel Osment 106
    Lynn Sear 108, 114-116, 122-124, 126
    M. Night Shyalaman 105
    Malcolm Crowe 106, 115, 116, 122, 126, 127
    Shyalaman 105
    Toni Collette 106
Slave narrative 14, 27
Smith, Kevin 5

134

Dogma 5
Southern womanhood 52
Stories or Tales from Olden Times 90
Sundance Kid 5
Sunset Boulevard 106

Tales of Mother Goose 90
Thelma and Louise .... ii, 5, 65, 68-71, 70-81
  Brad Pitt 69
  Callie Khouri 65
  Davis 68
  Geena Davis 1
  Hal Slocum 1
  JD 65, 68, 69
  Ridley Scott 65
  Susan Sarandon 68
Thompson, Kristin 1
To Wong Foo, Thanks for Everything! Julie Newmar .... ii, 5, 75, 95, 96, 98-100, 102
  Arliss Howard 96
  Bobby Lee 96, 97, 99, 100
  Bobby Ray 96, 97, 99, 100
  Carol Ann 96, 98, 99
  Chi Chi 96, 97, 99-102
  Chi Chi Rodriguez 95, 96
  John Leguizamo 95
  Julie Newmar 100
  Noxeema Jackson 75, 95-98, 100-102
  Patrick Swayze 95
  Sheriff Dollard 97-99, 102
  Snydersville 96, 98, 99, 102
  Stockard Channing 96
  Vida Boheme 95, 96
  Virgil 96, 98, 99, 102
  Wesley Snipes 95
Treasure of the Sierra Madre (The) 1
Turner, Ted 11
Twain, Mark (See also Samuel Clemens) 4, 12, 15-18, 23, 27
Vietnam 2
Wilson, Woodrow 47, 55, 58, 59, 61

STUDIES IN HISTORY AND CRITICISM OF FILM

1a. Bert Cardullo, **Practical Film Criticism–An Enlightened Approach to Moviegoing**, volume I

1b. Bert Cardullo, **Practical Film Criticism–An Enlightened Approach to Moviegoing**, volume II

2. Hans Joachim Meurer, **Cinema and National Identity in a Divided Germany, 1979-1989: The Split Screen**

3. Del Jacobs, **Revisioning Film Traditions–The Pseudo-Documentary and the NeoWestern**

4. Phebe Davidson, **American Movies and Their Cultural Antecedents in Literary Text**